Introdu

The Clwydian Range is a designal
Beauty, which includes Loggerhead
managed by Denbighshire Countryside
its impressive Iron Age hillforts offers
panoramic views. My first guidebook pro   ....ou to the
Offa's Dyke Path, generally covering the western side of the Range.

This second volume, now fully revised and extended, explores its many
other beautiful parts and less well known paths. In particular, it covers in
depth the large area of carboniferous limestone, which forms a significant
part of the Range. Formed millions of years ago when North Wales was
covered by a tropical sea, and, later tilted by major earth movements, the
exposed limestone escarpments, pavements, and outcrops, provide stunning
contrasting scenery to the lush green hills and valleys, and offer delightful walking. The area from Hendre to Llananarmon-y-Ial contained rich
seams of lead within the underlying limestone, and was extensively mined
between the 17th and 19th centuries. This industrial heritage is a backcloth
to many of the walks.

The 23 linked circular walks in this book feature open hills, impressive limestone countryside, attractive woodland, and the beautiful wooded
Alyn Valley with its famous 'leete path'. They follow old miners paths and
explore the Country Parks and new Open Access areas. They visit medieval
sites, ancient communities, lead-mining villages, nature reserves, and old
country inns.

The routes, which range from a 2 mile woodland trail to an exhilarating
8 mile upland walk incorporating two stunning hillforts, are well within
the capability of most people. Many routes contain shorter walk options.
A key feature is that individual walks can easily be linked with others to
provide longer and more challenging day walks if required. They follow
public rights of way or permissive paths, and cross Open Access land.
Walking boots are recommended, along with appropriate clothing to protect
against the elements. Please remember that the condition of the paths can
vary according to season and weather! Contact the relevant local Highways
Department or Countryside Service regarding any problems encountered
(see page 40 for details).

Each walk has a detailed map and description which enables the route
to be followed without difficulty, but be aware that changes in detail can
occur at any time. (e.g. new stile/field boundary). The location of each walk
is shown on the back cover and a summary of the key characteristics of each
is provided. This includes an estimated walking time, but allow more time
to enjoy the scenery. Most walks are accessible by local bus services.

Please observe the country code and respect any ancient site visited.
Enjoy your walking!

GWAENYSGOR & LLANASA

DESCRIPTION An 6¼ mile walk linking two attractive ancient settlements of Gwaenysgor and Llanasa, with their old churches and inviting inns, at the most northerly section of the Clwydian Range, offering breathtaking views of coast, sea, estuary, hills and mountains. The outward route includes a section of Offa's Dyke Path along the steep west-facing Prestatyn Hillside – a Site of Special Scientific Interest – whose panoramic views compensate for the subsequent effort to regain height. Allow about 3½ hours. The route can easily be undertaken as two shorter walks from respective villages, or varied using link roads. Binoculars are recommended.
START Gwaenysgor [SJ 075811] or Llanasa [SJ 106815].
DIRECTIONS Gwaenysgor is signposted from the A5151 just west of Trelawnyd. Roadside parking is available in the village centre. (For information on Gwaenysgor see **Walk 2**). Llanasa is signposted from the centre of Trelawnyd. A car park is available opposite the parish church.

I From the staggered crossroads head north through the village. Shortly, go along a no through road on the left by Eirianfa, then continue along an enclosed path to reach the village well – *the main source of water until after the First World War*. Follow the path ahead to a stile/kissing gate, through small trees and on across the lower slopes of the open gorse-covered hillside to cross a stile at a stunning viewpoint – *from the Clwyd delta along the coast to the Great Orme, and the mountains of Snowdonia beyond.*

2 Turn RIGHT to enjoy an exhilarating section of the Offa's Dyke Path along the edge of Prestatyn Hillside, before gradually descending past a quarry to a road – *enjoying good views of the coastal windfarm*. Go up the road and after passing a large green shelter, and just beyond a path angling down

on the left to a copper-domed house, turn RIGHT up a wide path through trees (or continue up the road to point **3**). Just beyond steps and before a bench-seat at a crossroad of paths, go up a stepped path to an access track. Turn RIGHT then LEFT up past the nearby house to a finger post. Go up the edge of a wood, then turn LEFT down a road.

3 On the bend, turn RIGHT to follow a signposted path up the wood edge to a stile into a field. Follow the boundary on the left to cross a nearby stile. Head half-RIGHT up the steep open slope – *enjoying extensive views from Snowdonia to Merseyside* – to cross a stile at the top. Head to a stile in the fence ahead, then angle up across the next large field to another stile. Go half-LEFT across the next field to a stile onto a track.

4 Follow the track LEFT soon bending past a Police radio mast. *Ahead are views across the mouth of the Dee Estuary to the distant Lancashire coast.* When the track bends left by a ruined house, turn RIGHT up the signposted bridleway along the edge of Acre Wood. After levelling out the enclosed bridleway passes a stile on the right access-

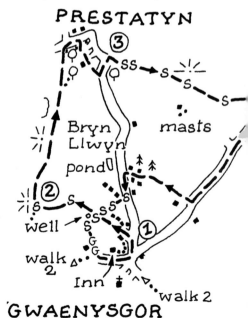

ing the return route at point 6, then continues across the hillside. *On a clear day the Lake District mountains and Blackpool Tower can be seen. Prominent on the shoreline is the former Talacre lighthouse.* After passing a house, continue along its access track. At a signposted byway, turn RIGHT past a good viewpoint across the Dee estuary towards Liverpool . Follow the hedge-lined lane to the road at Llanasa. Turn RIGHT, soon passing 17th C Henblas Hall to reach the Red Lion Inn.

L lanasa, with its pristine stone buildings, was founded around the church of the second Bishop of St Asaph. The church's east window is said to have come from Basingwerk Abbey upon its dissolution in the 16thC. In the graveyard are buried many people who have drowned in the nearby Dee estuary, including the crew of the Point of Air lifeboat who drowned on 4th January 1854 in heavy seas. Following this tragedy, crew were instructed to wear the new cork lifejackets, or risk a fine.

5 Take the road signposted to Gwaenysgor/ Trelawnyd, past the village pond, to leave Llanasa. Just before a small wood, take

LEFT up the next field to cross another stile. Continue in the same direction (ignore path leading to the wood corner). *Down to your left is Golden Grove – a stylish 16thC mansion originally the seat of the Morgan family.* Cross two stiles in the field corner by a small pond. Turn RIGHT..

6 Just before a stile in the corner, turn sharp LEFT to follow telegraph posts across the undulating field to cross two stiles at the top corner of a plantation. Continue alongside the wood edge to cross a stile by St Elmo's wood planted in 1994. *It takes its name from a summerhouse that once graced the top of the hillside, on a site also used by the Morgans as a pets graveyard.* Continue along the field edge towards the masts to cross a stile onto the track by your outward route. Follow it LEFT, soon steadily descending and becoming a lane. After one-third of a mile, turn RIGHT along a signposted enclosed bridleway to reach a road by Bryn Llwyn pond. Follow the road LEFT and shortly cross a stile on the right. Follow the waymarked path across two fields to reach the village well. Cross the stone stile opposite and follow the path to a ladder-stile, then

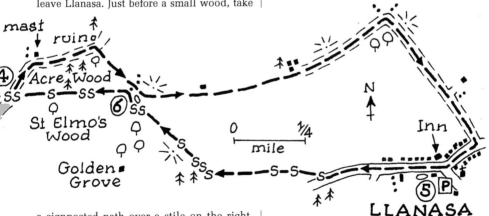

a signposted path over a stile on the right. Head half-LEFT up to a stile, angle up to another, then continue in the same direction up across the next large field to cross a stile in the top corner by a small plantation. Go up over two more stiles, then go half-

along the next field edge to a kissing gate. Keep ahead to another kissing gate, then turn LEFT up a track and follow the road past the Eagle and Child Inn in Gwaenysgor.

WALK 2
GOP HILL & MARIAN MILL

DESCRIPTION A 6 mile (**A**) or 5 mile (**B**) walk exploring undulating countryside and places of historical interest, with excellent views. After an easy climb to Gop Hill, with its ancient summit cairn on Gop Hill – the largest in Wales, the route visits the old settlement of Gwaenysgor, with its 12thC church and 19thC inn. It then follows an attractive section of the Offa's Dyke Path for nearly two miles to Marian Mill, before returning via old bridleways. Allow about 3 hours.
START High Street, Trelawnyd [SJ 091798] or Gwaenysgor [SJ 075811].
DIRECTIONS Trelawnyd lies on the A5151 road 2 miles east of Dyserth. In the village centre, by the war memorial and village hall, take the road signposted to Llanasa (High Street), where there is a car park on the right. See **Walk 1** for the alternative start.

*T*relawnyd is also known as 'Newmarket' – a name given it by the local entrepreneur John Wynne in 1700 after he enlarged the village and established a weekly market and four annual fairs. He promoted the trades of tanning, nail making, silk weaving and tobacco preparation, but none survived for long. The village economy still largely relied on farming and local lead-mining. The population peaked at 713 in 1841.

I Walk up High Street and follow the road out of the village to take a path on the left signposted Millennium Trail/ Gwaenysgor. Continue up to another stone stile/kissing gate. In the next field use the stile or kissing on the left, then keep ahead on the path signposted to Bryn Gop. The path soon rises gently through the wood, before rejoining the boundary at a prominent viewpoint. Continue along the wood edge, past an open area with extensive views, to reach the cairn on Gop Hill. Follow a path across its south-facing slope to the summit. *The purpose of the bronze age or early neolithic*

cairn (14 metres high and 100 metres wide) is uncertain. Legend associates it with Queen Boadicea's final resting place. Thought to be a burial mound, late 19thC excavations revealed no evidence of burials. However, the remains of 14 neolithic people buried in a crouched position have been found in a cave below the summit. The views are superb, ranging from Blackpool Tower to the mountains of Snowdonia.

2 Return down the path, then bear RIGHT down to a kissing-gate. Head half-LEFT down the hillside towards Trelawnyd to a finger post at a path junction. Here turn RIGHT and follow the wide level path across the mid-slopes of Gop Hill, passing above Gop Farm and a derelict 17thC stone dovecot to cross a stile at the bottom corner of a wood. Cross the nearby stile, then head down the middle of a large field, past a telegraph pole, to cross a stile ahead, and on over another stile in the next field corner onto a road. Follow it RIGHT into Gwaenysgor. In the village centre, turn LEFT to reach the Eagle and Child Inn.

*G*waenysgor is an ancient settlement, whose 12thC Church of St Mary Magdalene stands on an important pre-Roman religious site, denoted by its circular churchyard. It holds the only unbroken parish records in Wales dating from 1538. Dating from 1831, the Inn takes its name from the legend of a medieval nobleman who persuaded his wife to adopt his illegitimate child, alleging it had been found in an eagle's nest on his estate.

3 Continue along the lane and down a stony track to cross a stile by Ty Draw. Follow the waymarked stiled path through three fields. It then continues down alongside a fence – *enjoying panoramic views* – to cross two further stiles, then descends the part gorse-covered slope to join the Offa's Dyke Path. Turn LEFT and follow the waymarked National Trail (Acorn sign) as it contours along the hillside, past the edge of a quarry and side paths to eventually reach Red Roofs. Go along its access track to a road.

4 Turn LEFT, then LEFT again at the junction. Go up the road to cross a stile on the right at the entrance to Clarence House. Now follow the waymarked Offa's Dyke Path through several fields and down to a road. Follow it LEFT, then shortly cross a stile on your right. Head up the field and on down the next to reach the A5151. Turn RIGHT, then cross the road and a stile opposite. Follow the path to a minor road. Continue down the road past cottages – *note the ruin of Grove Mill below* – and on the bend continue ahead along a track signposted to Marian

Cwm to reach Marian Mill. *The fast flowing stream – a good source of watercress – once turned the waterwheels of these mills for generating power for turning corn into flour and for the fulling process in the preparation of yarns and woven fabric.* (For **Walk B** turn left past the house and follow the bridleway along the valley to rejoin the main walk.)

5 Bear RIGHT alongside old railings and at a small stone building, leave Offa's Dyke Path by continuing alongside the railings, then follow a hedge-lined bridleway to a road by Marian Mawr. Follow it LEFT past a junction, then just past Plasse Farm, cross a stile on the left. Head half-RIGHT across the large field. *The sheer scale of the summit cairn on Gop Hill can now be fully appreciated.* Cross a stile in the far boundary, then turn LEFT to follow a hedge-lined bridleway, later narrowing and being joined by Walk B near a stream. Follow the delightful narrow bridleway to a waymarked junction. Here, turn

LEFT, then soon cross a stile on the right and go through two fields to a lane. Follow it LEFT. *Ahead is the church of St Michael and All Angels, dating from 1724. On its south side is a 13thC preaching cross.* Shortly, turn RIGHT along the A5151 back to the start.

5

WALK 3
MOEL Y PARC [1]

DESCRIPTION Moel y Parc stands at the northern end of the central Clwydians. It is a large yet little known Open Access area, being traditional Common Land, offering extensive views. This meandering 5 mile walk, with options, uses a network of delightful green paths to reach its summit cairn (1296 feet) and to explore its southern slopes and adjoining foothill. Allow about 3 hours.

START Aberwheeler [SJ 096694].

DIRECTIONS Aberwheeler lies on the B5429. Park in a lay-by opposite Bro Lleweni.

1 At the nearby junction, turn LEFT. Just past Efail-y-waen farm, turn RIGHT and follow the minor road to Tyn y Celyn. Cross the stream and go up the track and through a gate on the left by Tyn y Celyn cottage. Go up two fields to join the Offa's Dyke Path at a finger post. Cross the nearby stile. Follow the fence on the left up to a bridleway. Follow it LEFT to a gate.

2 Here do a sharp U-turn up by the fence. At its corner keep ahead on a path rising across the bracken slope to a crossroad of paths by a tree. Keep ahead. The path rises then contours across the hillside, past a cross-path, to reach a path junction. Bear LEFT up the path. After 20 yards, turn LEFT and follow a wide green path up the hillside to eventually reach a path junction at a new viewpoint north. Turn RIGHT and follow the wide path up to a summit cairn. It now heads towards Moel y Parc. Take its undulating left fork to a waymarker post at a crossroad of paths. Follow the path ahead up to Moel y Parc's summit cairn.

3 Do a sharp U-turn right waymarked to Penycloddiau. Options: **Route A:** take a rougher path bisecting the two main waymarked paths,

descending in stages above the bracken covered side valley. At a crossroad of paths, turn RIGHT down the bracken hillside. **Route B:** follow the ridge path alongside the fence, soon descending. At a double section of fence take a path angling down through bracken to join Route A. (**Route C:** continue down the ridge. Just before a gate, turn right and follow the boundary down.)

4 At a fence corner you have options to point 5. **Route A:** keep ahead (SW) with the wide path, soon steadily descending to join Offa's Dyke Path. Follow the track down to pass a farm and up to a finger post. Continue up the stony track (bridleway). When it bends right, go up a farm track ahead alongside a boundary. **Route B:** take a path NW, initially near an old boundary, down to cross a stream. Go half-left to join a bridleway by a gate. Continue down the track past cottages. On the bend keep ahead up a farm track.

5 Continue with a path, keeping to its left fork, to join your outward route. Go down its left fork. At another path junction keep ahead descending to join a bridleway/O.D. Path at a finger post. Take the O.D. Path down to cross a stile on your outward route. Now follow the stiled O.D. Path down through fields to join the road at Grove Goch. Return by road to Aberwheeler.

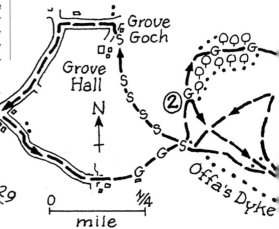

WALK 4

MOEL Y PARC [2]

DESCRIPTION For experienced walkers a 4¾ mile (**A**) or 4½ mile (**B**) walk exploring Moel y Parc's little visited wilder slopes. Route A contours around its northern slopes overlooking the Wheeler valley; Route B crosses its second top. From its summit cairn (1296 feet) both routes return via an attractive foothill. Allow about 3½ hours..

START As **Walk 3**.

1 Follow instructions in paragraph **1** of **Walk 3**.

2 Go through the gate. Shortly take the bridleway's right fork up to a gate. After another gate the bridleway rises up the attractive side valley, later bending left. It then bends right.

Route A: after 10 yards take a path briefly alongside the fence on your left. Follow the path across the hillside,

then as it begins to descend, take a fainter path rising to the right. Continue across the slope then follow an intermittent path NNW, maintaining height, to eventually pass a large boulder with views across the Wheeler valley. Just before an old wall, head up the slope to a cairn on an outlying flank at the wall's highest point. Follow the wall for 20 yards, then turn RIGHT up to a cross-path. Follow it LEFT (NE) through gorse – *now with views down to large quarry pools*. Continue across the northern slopes, maintaining height. Later head towards the transmitter mast to reach two trees at the top of an expansive side valley. Descend the nearby stream to a cross-path by another tree. Follow it up the slope towards the mast. When it fades keep ahead through heather to soon reach a cross-path. Follow it RIGHT, then just before it rises, turn LEFT along another path towards the mast, following its right fork to reach a wide cross-path after 100 yards. Follow it RIGHT up to the summit cairn.

Route B: on the bridleway's next bend, take a path LEFT up and across the bracken slope, soon rising steadily. Continue up its right fork, then across the hillside, joining another path angling in from the left and briefly rising. When it splits keep ahead, soon overlooking a small ridge with a cairn. Bear RIGHT then head SE up the hillside towards the mast (various sheep tracks) to join a good path crossing the broad undulating heather-covered top past large crags. The path heads towards Penycloddiau, then gently descends a small craggy slope to reach a cross-path overlooking a side valley. Follow it LEFT towards the mast to reach the summit cairn.

3 Take the wide path signposted to Aifft down the hillside to a waymarker post at a cross-road of paths. Follow the undulating path ahead to a cairn on a small unnamed top. The wide path now steadily descends. At a path junction, keep straight ahead down a narrower path to eventually pass a large boulder to reach a bridleway. Keep ahead to join a path by the fence below to cross a familiar stile. Now follow the stiled Offa's Dyke Path down through fields to Grove Goch. Return by road to Aberwheeler.

WALK 5

BRYN GOLAU & YSCEIFIOG LAKE

DESCRIPTION A delightful 6½ mile walk exploring the contrasting scenery on both sides of the Wheeler valley. The route first heads south to meander around and across the foothill of Bryn Golau, reaching a height of 918 feet and enjoying good views, before heading north to the ancient village of Ysceifiog, with its traditional country inn. It than passes the attractive Ysceifiog Lake hidden in delightful woodland, finishing at Y Ddol Uchaf wetland and woodland nature reserve. Allow about 3½ hours. The route can be undertaken as two shorter walks using a link section of road.

START Lay-by on A541 near Afonwen [SJ 143711] or Ysceifiog [SJ 152716].

DIRECTIONS Park in either of two lay-bys situated ¾ mile east of Afonwen on the A541 Mold-Denbigh road. For the alternative start, turn off the A541 to Ysceifiog, where roadside parking is available.

I Take the minor road located between the lay-bys heading south. Shortly, take a side road on the left. It rises steadily, then continues – *with good views across the Wheeler valley* – past a bridleway/driveway to Plas Gwyn. After passing Tyn y Pwll, the road rises. Soon do a sharp 'U'-turn to follow a signposted bridleway along a track. *Prominent to the north is Ysceifiog church.* Go past a cottage, then take the left fork of the track to pass just above a house. The green track then rises through a waymarked gate and continues steadily up the edge of upland pasture alongside a fence – *soon with a view of Moel y Parc with its TV transmitter mast, and Penycloddiau further south.*

2 When the track levels out and fades, angle away from the fence to follow a path contouring across the hillside to join the boundary on the right which you follow to go through a gate. Continue ahead, soon alongside another tree/fence boundary to pass above the farm. At the boundary corner keep ahead through gorse, over a stile and on through a gate by a small plantation. Continue down the farm's access track past Bishopsfield, then at another house follow the signposted bridleway along the lane ahead to pass Hen Living. Just beyond a wood, take the signposted bridleway along the left fork of the track, soon passing through a gate and continuing along the Disgynfa valley. After passing a track to a cottage the track forks.

3 Here cross a stile on the left and head half-LEFT up and across the field to a gate in the corner. Follow the boundary on the left through the next two fields, rising to a stile at a good viewpoint. Continue ahead across the next two open fields, then go along a delightful stiled tree-lined path, and down through trees to pass a former Methodist chapel. Continue down its access track/ lane to a road. Follow it down to cross over the former Mold – Denbigh railway line and river Wheeler at Sarn to reach the A541.

4 Go up the road opposite, signposted to Ysceifiog, then take a signposted bridleway up a track on the right past houses to reach a lane. Follow it LEFT , then take a signposted path over a stile on the right. Go ahead along the field edge and through a strip of woodland, then go half-LEFT up the field to go through the left of two gates. Now follow the stiled field path to enter the corner of 19thC St Mary's churchyard by a 'gravestone' stile. *Nearby are the remains of an old preaching cross.* Leave the churchyard by the main gate and head down towards the Fox Inn – an 18thC traditional country inn.

Ysceifiog, a remote, tiny, and ancient settlement set 600ft above sea-level, and mentioned in the Doomsday Book, has an interesting history. It developed mainly as an agricultural community, but has prospered from its diversity of natural resources. Limestone, lead ore, sand and gravel have been worked here. An iron ore mine once supplied Brymbo Ironworks. Mills were established along the Pant Gwyn stream. Wool manufacturing developed and houses were built for cotton pickers in 1792. Interestingly, Guy Fawkes stopped at Ysceifiog on his way to Holywell, shortly before the Gunpowder Plot, and witches were reported in the parish as late as 1938.

In 1816, one of Britain's finest bronze age gold circular torques was found a mile from Ysceifiog – a collar of twisted gold 50 inches long, 14 inches wide, 20 oz in weight, of Irish origin – traditionally worn round the neck by chieftains as an insignia of power.

5 Turn RIGHT past the village hall to the junction. Turn LEFT. The road steadily descends – *providing a first view of Ysceifiog lake in its deep wooded valley with Moel y Parc beyond. Just past Drovers Tumble,* cross a stream and take a path on the left signposted to Babell/Caerwys. *This delightful path accompanies the Pant Gwyn stream along the edge*

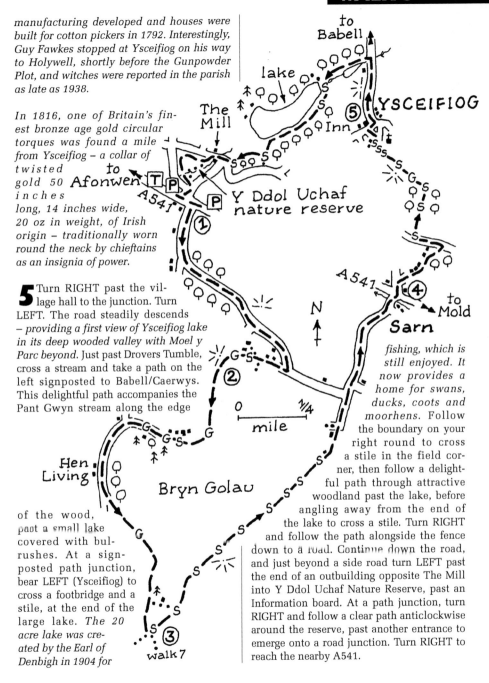

of the wood, past a small lake covered with bulrushes. At a signposted path junction, bear LEFT (Ysceifiog) to cross a footbridge and a stile, at the end of the large lake. *The 20 acre lake was created by the Earl of Denbigh in 1904 for*

fishing, which is still enjoyed. It now provides a home for swans, ducks, coots and moorhens. Follow the boundary on your right round to cross a stile in the field corner, then follow a delightful path through attractive woodland past the lake, before angling away from the end of the lake to cross a stile. Turn RIGHT and follow the path alongside the fence down to a road. Continue down the road, and just beyond a side road turn LEFT past the end of an outbuilding opposite The Mill into Y Ddol Uchaf Nature Reserve, past an Information board. At a path junction, turn RIGHT and follow a clear path anticlockwise around the reserve, past another entrance to emerge onto a road junction. Turn RIGHT to reach the nearby A541.

WALK 6
CWM DISGYNFA

DESCRIPTION A 5¼ mile walk around the attractive Disgynfa valley and across the lower eastern slopes of Penycloddiau, reaching a height of 1066 feet. Allow about 2½ hours.
START Lay-by on A541 near Afonwen [SJ 143711].
DIRECTIONS See **Walk 5**.

I Take the minor road located between the lay-bys heading south. Follow the road up the valley for 1⅓ miles to its end by large farm buildings and the entrance to Cimwch farm. Go up the tree-lined stony track to a gate, then follow the green track up the hillside to another gate. Turn LEFT through a nearby gate and follow the signposted path along the edge of upland pasture to a further gate, then down through bracken to a stile/gate. The path now follows the old wall on your left through gorse and occasionally wet terrain beneath Penycloddiau, later rising to a stile and continuing past a ruin to a stile/ sleeper bridge. Bear LEFT down the long reedy field to a stile at the bottom. After crossing another stile ahead follow a narrowing path through trees then ahead along a green track.

2 At a track junction bear LEFT and follow the enclosed track (a bridleway) to a gate. Continue across open ground to join a lane. Follow it to a large white house. Here, turn LEFT over a cattle grid and down the lane. On the bend at the entrance to Maes y Esgob, cross a stile and follow the signposted path along the field edge to another stile. Go along the top of the field to cross a large footbridge in the recessed corner. Go up through the trees to cross a stile. Turn LEFT along the wood/field edge, then continue beside the boundary to eventually go through a gate in the field corner and another further ahead. Go down the track to a stile/gate above a house. Just beyond do a sharp U-turn to follow the access

track (a bridleway) down past Plas Gwyn to the road. Follow it LEFT down to join your outward route.

10

WALK 7
BRYN GOLAU

DESCRIPTION A 5¼ mile walk exploring the hills and valleys near Nannerch, following old tracks, bridleways, paths and quiet country roads. The route first descends to Melin-y-Wern, then follows a delightful river valley, crosses the open hill of Bryn Golau (918 feet), and returns past an ancient house. Allow about 3 hours.
START Nannerch [SJ 166696].
DIRECTIONS Nannerch lies just off the A541. Park tidily in the village centre.

1 Go north along Village Road past the 19thC church, then turn LEFT along Ffordd y Waen. Shortly take the signposted hedge-lined byway on the right, later descending past outbuildings of a cottage and continuing to a lane. Follow it LEFT to a T-junction. Take the signposted stiled path

2 At a junction, turn LEFT. At the next continue up the No Through road, then follow the waymarked bridleway up a track to a former Methodist chapel. Continue on the bridleway up through trees to a stile, then go along a delightful stiled tree-lined path and across two open fields to a stile at a good viewpoint. Now follow the tree boundary on the right down to another stile and through the next field to a waymarked gate/stile near the corner. Go ahead across the field towards Penycloddiau, shortly descending to the right of gorse to a stile by holly trees onto a green track junction.

3 Here bend sharp LEFT and follow the hedge/tree-lined track past a cottage to eventually reach a lane. Follow it RIGHT. When it becomes two access tracks at a finger post, go through a gate up on the left. Go through the field to cross a stream and go through a gate. Go up the field edge, then angle across to a stile/gate onto a road. Follow it RIGHT, then at the junction turn LEFT. The road soon rises then continues towards Nannerch. Later it passes Walgoch – *an ancient stone house and farm.* Take a signposted path through a gate opposite its last barn. Go half-RIGHT across the field to its far edge beyond a large metal cylinder. Continue along the wooded edge overlooking Nannerch, then descend through trees to a stile at the corner of a children's play area. Descend the pathway, then continue ahead along the road. On the bend, keep ahead to follow a pathway to Village Road – and perhaps a drink at the 18thC Cross Foxes Inn.

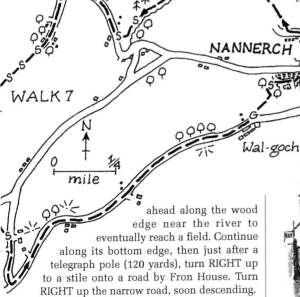

ahead along the wood edge near the river to eventually reach a field. Continue along its bottom edge, then just after a telegraph pole (120 yards), turn RIGHT up to a stile onto a road by Fron House. Turn RIGHT up the narrow road, soon descending.

WALK 8

MOEL ARTHUR & PENYCLODDIAU

DESCRIPTION An exhilarating 8 mile walk (**A**) exploring the beautiful, yet little known, eastern valleys and foothills of the Clwydians, featuring two stunning Iron-Age hillforts and ever changing views. Allow about 4 – 5 hours. The route can easily be undertaken as two shorter circuits of 4¼ (**B**) or 5¼ (**C**) miles using the link road.
START Llangwyfan Forestry car park [SJ 139668].
DIRECTIONS From Mold, take the A541 towards Denbigh, then turn off left for Nannerch. Take the first road left, signposted Llandyrnog, for about 3 miles to the car park at the top of the pass.

For **Walk B**, follow the road north down to point **4**. For the main walk follow the road RIGHT then take the signposted Offa's Dyke Path (Moel Arthur) on the left to a stile. Climb up the steep grassy slope to cross two further stiles. The path now rises less steeply to reach the shoulder of Moel Arthur. At a slate waymarker, turn RIGHT to follow a path to the top of the hill through the original fort entrance.

The conical heather-covered hill of Moel Arthur (1494 ft) is crowned by a small, but prominent Iron-Age hillfort, defended on the naturally weaker northern side by two impressive ramparts and ditches. There is evidence of hut circles, and a hoard of Bronze Age copper axes have been found here.
Retrace your steps to follow Offa's Dyke Path down to a road in the next valley.

2 Turn LEFT along the road. Shortly turn RIGHT along a track to a facing stile/gate. Follow the track along the forest edge beneath Moel Llys-y-coed. After a gate the enclosed track continues beyond the forest corner, later rising. Take a signposted byway through a gate on the left. Go along the tree-lined stony track, later passing a signed bridleway and gradually descending. Just beyond an old corrugated barn, cross a stile on the left. Keep ahead along the field edge then angle down to a stile. Angle RIGHT down the next field to a waymarked fence just beyond old stone gateposts. Follow it LEFT, over a stream, and on to cross a stile in the fence. Follow the path LEFT down to cross the stream, and a stile opposite. Just beyond bear LEFT up across the field, passing between two trees to cross a hidden stile in the tree boundary ahead. Angle up the next field, past a telegraph pole to a stile onto a road. Turn LEFT, then cross a stile on your right.

3 Continue ahead by the old boundary, soon descending to cross a stile in the fence corner. Angle LEFT to cross a stream and another further ahead by a tree to reach a fence corner beyond. Cross the stream and follow the fence up the field to go through a waymarked facing gate in the top corner. Follow the waymarked track along the forest edge, soon descending steadily, then bending past outbuildings to a gate. The track now passes a cottage, and continues up to meet another track at a finger post. Here do a sharp U-turn and continue up the delightful tree-lined track. After passing through a gate just beyond a ruined cottage, head half-RIGHT up across upland pasture, soon levelling out – *with good views of Penycloddiau and Moel y Parc*. Continue in the same direction, soon descending steadily the large field towards Penycloddiau to go through a waymarked gate in the corner. Follow the fence round to cross a stile. Now, go half-LEFT across the upland pasture, soon descending to cross a stile ahead. Follow a green track down near the fence. At a waymarker post cross a stile to the right above Bryn-ffynnon farm. Descend between gorse to go through a small wooden gate by an outbuilding, and on over a stile, then follow the driveway to the road.

4 Take the signposted path through the gate opposite, and follow the boundary on the left. At its corner, turn LEFT over a stream and continue to cross a stile and another stream ahead. Go up the field edge, over a stile, then up the right-hand side of an old tree boundary to go through a waymarked gateway above. Follow the boundary on the right up the field to cross a stile ahead. Continue up the next field edge, past a house, to cross a stile in the corner. Follow the path down to a fence corner, then descend the short steep slope to cross a footbridge and stile below. Follow the old field boundary, then just before old stone gateposts, angle LEFT up the gorse-covered slope ahead to cross a hidden stile in a

fence corner. Follow the fence up the slope, through a gateway at the top, and on across level ground.

5 In the field corner follow the fence bearing LEFT round to cross a stile into Open Access land. Now follow the old embanked walled boundary on your right, past a ruin, and on to cross a stile. Continue with the old wall down and across wettish ground to a stile/gate, then follow the green path up through bracken to a gate and along the edge of upland pasture to another gate onto a green cross track. Follow it LEFT. Go past a farm entrance, then when the stony track bends right, cross a stile on the left to rejoin Offa's Dyke Path. Head half-LEFT up the slope past a clump of Scots pines, and simply follow the superb well waymarked ridge path rising steadily to the summit of Penycloddiau, with its Iron-Age fort, before continuing on a gradual descent back to the start.

*P*enycloddiau *(1443 feet) means 'The hill of the trenches'. Its hillfort is the largest on the Clwydians and one of the largest in Wales. Its interior is ½ mile long and it encloses an area of some 24 hectares, within a single substantial grass-covered rampart, strengthened at its northern end.*

WALK 9

MOEL PLAS-YW

DESCRIPTION This 5 mile walk, with excellent views, rises steadily from the Wheeler valley on an attractive old enclosed byway, before following an open green track to the high pass beneath Moel Arthur and Moel Llys-y-Coed. It then returns across the open slopes of Moel Plas-yw, reaching a height of 1279 feet, before descending to pass through the attractive Penbedw estate. Allow about 3 hours. The walk includes an optional extension to the Iron-Age fort on Moel Arthur.

START Lay-by on A541 Mold – Denbigh road. [SJ 680173] or alternatively the car park beneath Moel Arthur [SJ 148658].

DIRECTIONS From Mold take the A541 towards Denbigh. After about 6 miles, shortly after passing the turn-off for Cilcain and another minor road by a lodge, park in a lay-by on the left. For the alternative start, follow the minor road to the top of the pass beneath Moel Arthur.

I From the lay-by walk east along the road towards Mold, using available pavements. *In the field adjoining the lay-by, near some trees are the remains of a stone circle. Its origin is still uncertain.* At the lodge, turn RIGHT along the minor road, then take a signposted path over a stile on the left. Go half-RIGHT across the field to a stile onto another road. (If the path is blocked by maize continue to the next road signposted to Cilcain.) At the first bend, take the signposted byway past the entrance to Tardd-y-dwr. Continue up the lane, which later becomes a track. Just past Siamber Wen, when the track splits, take the right fork. Continue along the narrow hedge-lined track, which can be muddy. It soon begins a long steady ascent, becoming more stony in character and tree-lined, to eventually go through a gate at its end onto a green cross track. Turn RIGHT and follow the track across open country – *with good views north to Halkyn Mountain, with Moel Plas-yw prominent.* The track then rises and passes alongside the edge of a forest – *later with Moel Arthur appearing ahead* – to eventually reach a minor road at the high pass lying between Moel Llys-y-Coed and Moel Arthur.

*F**or** those those with time and energy to spare, wishing to extend the walk to take in nearby Moel Arthur with its Iron-Age fort, follow the road left to the car park, then take the waymarked Offa's Dyke Path to the shoulder of Moel Arthur, then follow a path left to go through the original entrance of the fort to the summit. See Walk 8 for further information. Retrace your steps to resume the main walk.*

2 Turn RIGHT along the road, and after about 100 yards, go through a gate on the left by a finger post. Follow the green track rising steadily up the hillside – *soon enjoying good views down the part wooded valley, north – east towards Merseyside, and east to Beeston and Peckforton hills in Cheshire, and on a clear day the Pennines beyond.* The track then levels out before descending and crossing the western slopes of Moel Plas-yw – *with new views: west over the Vale of Clwyd and Denbigh Moors to the mountains of Snowdonia; north-west to nearby Penycloddiau, with its Iron-Age fort, and Moel y Parc with its TV transmitter mast; and north to the coast.*

3 After crossing a stile by a gate at the end of the track, continue ahead across open pasture near an old embanked boundary on your left. Shortly, follow a green track past a small wood, over a stile by a gate, and on down to pass through a gate near a ruined cottage. Continue down the track through a delightful avenue of majestic mature trees – *later with fine views across open undulating countryside towards Mold, and Moel Famau, with its ruined Jubilee Tower – the highest point in the Clwydian Range, but looking less imposing from this viewpoint.* When it meets another track, keep ahead, descending to pass over a cattle-grid. *Ahead lie the various buildings of Penbedw. The original grand 18thC Penbedw Hall became derelict and was demolished in 1958.* Continue down the track to pass the front of an elegant house. After a gateway, turn RIGHT down its driveway and follow it to the A541. *In the lower part of the field to your right is a tumulus*

14

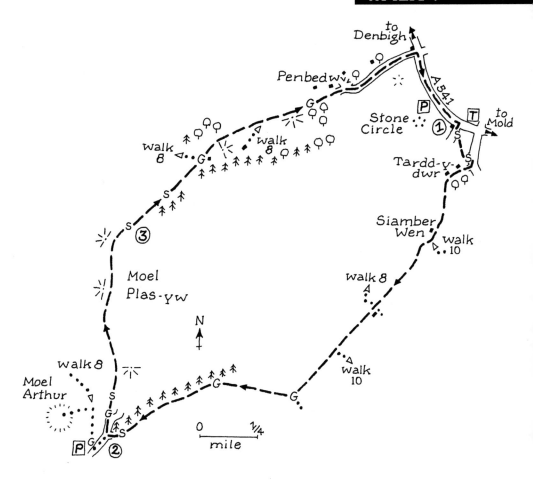

to
Denbigh

Penbedw

Stone
Circle

① P

T to
Mold

A541

Tardd-y-
dwr

walk
8

walk
8

G

Siamber
Wen

walk
10

Moel
Plas-yw

walk 8

N

walk 8

Moel
Arthur

walk
10

G

G

G

0   ¼
mile

P ②

– *an ancient burial site which revealed a burial urn when opened in 1860. At the road* turn RIGHT and walk WITH CARE along the road edge back to the start.

About the author.....

David is an experienced walker with a love of the countryside and an interest in local history. He is the author of a series of walks guidebooks covering North Wales, where he has lived and worked for many years, as well as a freelance writer for Walking Wales magazine. He has worked as a Rights of Way surveyor across North Wales and has served as a member of Denbighshire Local Access Forum.

Whether on a riverside ramble, mountain or long distance walk, he greatly appreciates the beauty, culture and history of the landscape and hopes that his comprehensive guidebooks will encourage people to explore on foot its diverse scenery and rich heritage.

ALYN VALLEY & COED DDU

DESCRIPTION A 7¾ mile walk from Hendre or a 6¼ mile walk from Cilcain (starting from point **4**) exploring the attractive varied countryside between these small communities, with the opportunity of visiting their traditional old inns. From the 17thC Royal Oak in Hendre, the route rises in stages to the ancient hillside settlement of Cilcain with its medieval church and 16thC inn. It then visits the narrow wooded Alyn valley before returning through the attractive woodland of Coed Ddu and past a woodland reserve. Allow about 4¼ hours and 3½ hours respectively. The Alyn valley and adjoining limestone area became a major part of the lead-mining industry of NE Wales from the 17th to the 19th centuries.
START The Royal Oak, Hendre [SJ 189677] or Cilcain [SJ 177652].
DIRECTIONS The Royal Oak lies on the A541 about 5 miles west of Mold. Parking is allowed in the car park, but the landlord will appreciate being informed in advance. (tel. 01352 741466). *Please park tidily.*

I From the Royal Oak – *once used as a Coroners Court following the death of miners at Cilcain* – go to the nearby side road, then walk between Tollbar and Oak cottages to follow a path through the trees and past old quarry structures. Continue on a bridleway along the edge of a wood, past a lime kiln and Ty-isaf – *an old hall house* – and follow its access track to a road.

2 Go up the signposted byway opposite, then at Hilltop, continue along the narrow hedge-lined way, later widening. At a track junction near a farm turn LEFT along the hedge-lined track. (The initial section can be muddy after rain.) Shortly, it begins a long steady ascent, becoming more stony and tree-lined in character. It passes a signposted path on the left below an old barn. (This is an alternative stiled field path to point **3**). Eventually take a signposted bridleway on

the left. Follow this delightful bridleway to a road. Follow the road down to a junction. Turn RIGHT.

3 Follow the road down past the farm and up to another junction. Keep ahead and on the next bend cross a stile by the pumping station. Now follow the waymarked stiled path through fields to reach the village hall and road at Cilcain. *St Mary's 14thC church opposite contains a magnificent carved oak roof with winged angels, and is well worth a visit.* Turn LEFT to the White Horse – *a 16thC coaching inn. A piece of gold found in the nearby hills in 1889, created a short-lived 'gold rush' with several tiny mines opening. Sadly, one owned by the inn landlord failed to make him rich, being worked out after only 6 months!*

4 From the crossroads, follow the road signposted to Pantymwyn out of the village. After ½ mile, the road descends to a junction by Wallacre. Turn LEFT, then take a signposted path over a stile on the right. Follow the boundary on your left, through a gateway, soon descending the next field to cross a stile in the bottom corner. Go half-RIGHT across the field down to a stile onto a track (bridleway). Go up the enclosed path opposite, through a gate, and on past outbuildings and a cottage, then follow its access track to a lane. Immediately go down another track, then take a path passing beneath the gate to Pandy down through the trees. When it bends right down towards the river Alyn, take another waymarked path on the left through the wood, soon descending to cross a large footbridge over the river. *Ahead is the imposing limestone cliff of Pandy quarry which closed in 1950. It was originally the site of the great ironmaster John Wilkinson's Llyn y Pandy lead-mine, which he took over in 1791. The mine, which attracted Cornish workers, produced good yields of lead, which was probably shipped to his lead piping factory in London. However flooding remained a constant problem despite the efforts of four large steam engines, and contributed to its demise.* Turn LEFT to follow a path, soon joining a rising track. When above two cottages, take a waymarked track angling up through the trees. After about 150 yards, take a waymarked path on the left, following the lower of two paths down through the trees to join a track above the river and a caravan site. Follow it to cross a bridge over the river to join a road. Briefly keep ahead.

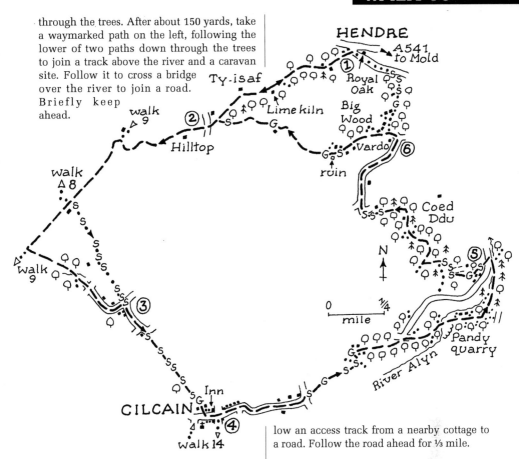

5 Take the signposted path angling back on the left up through trees, over a stile, and on up to a small gate. Continue ahead past a cottage, following the waymarked path to cross a stile. Cross the access track and a stile beyond. Go along the field edge and over a stile to enter Coed Ddu. *A house of the same name nearby is where, in 1829, the composer Mendelson stayed as guest of John Taylor, the mining engineer.* Follow a part-stepped path up through the wood to a waymarked crosspath. Follow it RIGHT through the trees, later descending to a multi-waymarked path junction. Take the path straight ahead up to another post, then bear RIGHT to follow a waymarked stony path past a ruined cottage, soon rising to a stile. Keep ahead through young trees, over another stile and on to fol-low an access track from a nearby cottage to a road. Follow the road ahead for ⅓ mile.

6 Just past Vardo, as the road begins to descend, take a signposted bridleway up a track on the left (soon passing a waymarked path/track offering a short cut to Hendre) to reach Big Wood owned by the Woodland Trust. Continue along the track to its end at the entrance to Mwynbwll Farm. Cross a stile by a gate ahead, then follow a faint green track to pass to the right of a ruin, down through trees to go through a gate ahead. Continue ahead, soon passing through trees, to follow a delightful meandering enclosed bridleway. After passing a house it begins a long steady descent to reach a finger post by a track. (For Cilcain continue along the track to the road at point **2**.) For Hendre, turn RIGHT to return along your outward route for a welcome drink at the Royal Oak.

WALK 11

MOEL FAMAU & MOEL DYWYLL

DESCRIPTION An exhilarating and varied 7¾ mile walk to Moel Famau (1820 ft) and Moel Dywyll using less well known paths. After rising in stages to Ffrith Mountain the route continues through Coed Moel Famau up to the Jubilee Tower. After a section of Offa's Dyke ridge path, it crosses the eastern slopes of Moel Dywyll, then returns via a delightful hillside track. Allow about 5 hours.

START Viewpoint car park west of Cilcain [SJ 169652].

DIRECTIONS Heading south from the A541 towards Cilcain, just before the village turn right on a signposted 'viewpoint'. Follow the minor road up past side roads to eventually reach crossroads. Turn left to reach two formal parking areas.

1 Head east. After the second parking area the road descends. At the first house on the right, go through the adjoining way-marked gate. Go ahead along the field edge – with a good view to Moel Famau – soon descending to a gateway. Descend the steep wooded slope to go through a gate at the end of a house. Go down the road and at the junction, turn LEFT past the Welsh Water building and follow the road past cottages. Just beyond a junction, go up a track on the right alongside Y Pentre and through a waymarked gate on the left. Go along the edge of two fields up to a stile. Go up the next field to an old stone stile in the recessed corner. Follow the stiled path along the edge of the next three fields to a gate, then up two further fields into a small wood. Follow the waymarked path up through trees to a track/bridleway.

2 Follow it LEFT to a gate above Ffrith farm. Continue ahead along the track past houses to a minor road. Follow it RIGHT to the entrance to Brithdir Mawr. Go along the track ahead on the waymarked bridleway, passing above the 16thC hall house. After a stile/gate continue along the track, then after 50 yards take a faint green track angling off on the right. When it fades continue up and across Ffrith Mountain's lower slopes to an old gateway. Continue up towards a distant finger post at the top forest/field corner, where you cross a stile.

3 Go through the adjoining bridle gate into Coed Moel Famau and down the multi-user track. It then rises through the open forest, later bending south east. At a signed cross-path at a good viewpoint, turn RIGHT. Follow the path up the heather-covered hillside, briefly descending then rising more steeply up the part forested slope to eventually reach the ruined Jubilee Tower at the top of Moel Famau. From the west side of the tower, take the main ridge Offa's Dyke Path signposted to Moel Arthur, then Moel Dywyll, soon passing a bench, and steadily descending. At the bottom of the slope the Offa's Dyke Path crosses a permissive bridleway, then continues along the ridge. At a signposted path junction, cross a stile on the right. Follow the path through heather past a small reedy pool then take a side path on the left (Tir Gofal).

4 Take the left fork and follow the path contouring across the heather-covered upper slopes of Moel Dywyll, later heading back to the ridge boundary. Keep with the upper left fork (the other is a lower alternative) continuing beneath the boundary to eventually reach a stony track. Turn RIGHT and follow this meandering track across the hillside. Later it becomes enclosed and reaches a house. Follow its access lane to crossroads, then turn RIGHT back to the start.

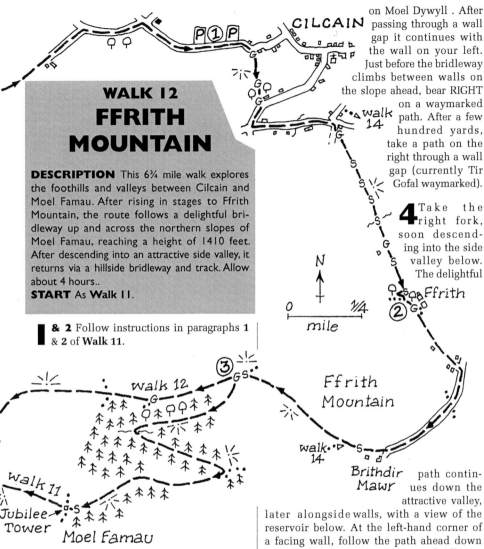

WALK 12
FFRITH MOUNTAIN

DESCRIPTION This 6¾ mile walk explores the foothills and valleys between Cilcain and Moel Famau. After rising in stages to Ffrith Mountain, the route follows a delightful bridleway up and across the northern slopes of Moel Famau, reaching a height of 1410 feet. After descending into an attractive side valley, it returns via a hillside bridleway and track. Allow about 4 hours..

START As **Walk 11**.

1 & 2 Follow instructions in paragraphs **1 & 2** of **Walk 11**.

3 Follow the signposted bridleway west up past an area of cleared forest, through a gate and on to a multi-finger post at the forest corner. Keep ahead on the signposted bridleway across the heather-covered hillside, soon with a wall on the right, then joined by one on the left. Ahead is the small cairn

on Moel Dywyll . After passing through a wall gap it continues with the wall on your left. Just before the bridleway climbs between walls on the slope ahead, bear RIGHT on a waymarked path. After a few hundred yards, take a path on the right through a wall gap (currently Tir Gofal waymarked).

4 Take the right fork, soon descending into the side valley below. The delightful path continues down the attractive valley, later alongside walls, with a view of the reservoir below. At the left-hand corner of a facing wall, follow the path ahead down past old fence posts to join a cross-bridleway just above an old wall. Follow it LEFT up the edge of the valley to join a stony track. Turn RIGHT and follow this meandering track across the hillside. Later it becomes enclosed and reaches a house. Follow its access lane to crossroads, then turn RIGHT back to the start.

MOEL FAMAU

DESCRIPTION A 5 mile (**A**) or 4¾ mile (**B**) meandering walk following delightful upland bridleways to Moel Famau (1820 ft), returning by a choice of routes. After a section of Offa's Dyke Path, **Walk A** crosses the heather-covered hillside then descends via a reservoir into the valley. **Walk B** descends a less well known path into an attractive side valley to a large reservoir and continues along the valley past others. Allow about 3 hours. The route can easily be shortened to a 3 mile walk (**C**)

START Waterworks ⅓ mile south west of Cilcain [SJ 172648].

DIRECTIONS From the village centre, go past the White Horse Inn, then turn left by the church. Follow the minor road down to park near waterworks.

I From the bend of the road go up the driveway to Tyddyn-y-foel, then after a few yards cross a stone stile on the right. Follow the stiled path up the edge of two fields to reach a track junction. Turn LEFT to follow the signposted bridleway up a track to a gate by a stream, and on up the hillside to pass through another gate. Continue straight ahead, soon crossing a boggy area by a raised wooden walkway. The delightful waymarked bridleway now contours round the hillside – *providing open views across to Cilcain, Halkyn Mountain and east towards Cheshire* – via a stile/gate to eventually go through a gate by a corrugated building. Go past the cottage and through the gate ahead, then continue along its green access track.

2 At a finger post, just before a gate ahead, do a sharp U-turn onto the signposted bridleway to Moel Famau. The bridleway rises through trees to a stile/gate, then begins a long steady ascent across the open slopes of Ffrith Mountain – *later with Moel Famau coming into view*. After passing a finger post the bridleway continues up past an area of cleared forest, later levelling out to go through a gate. (A nearby stile offers a link path to the main ascent path.) Continue ahead to reach a

finger post at the forest corner. (For **Walk C** turn right.) Turn LEFT on the signposted path to begin the final ascent to the Jubilee Tower at the top of Moel Famau.

*M*oel Famau, *meaning 'Mother's mountain', is the highest point in the Clwydian range. The Jubilee Tower was built in 1810 by public subscription to commemorate George III's 50 years as king. The original 115 foot tower, designed by Thomas Harrison of Chester and the first Egyptian-style monument to be built in Britain, must have been one of the most striking sights in North Wales. Only the base remains, the obelisk having been blown down by storms on 27th October 1862. The views are breathtaking – see the metal information boards.*

3 From the west side of the tower, take the main ridge Offa's Dyke Path signposted to Moel Arthur, then Moel Dywyll, soon passing a bench, and steadily descending. At the bottom of the slope the Offa's Dyke Path crosses a permissive bridleway, then continues along the ridge. At a signposted path junction, cross a stile on the right. Follow the path through heather past a small reedy pool.

4 At a side path on the left (currently way-marked Tir Gofal) you have a choice. For **Walk A** keep ahead with the main path. Just before a facing wall angle LEFT to join a bridleway which continues beneath the wall. After a short walled section, the bridleway continues to the multi-finger post at the forest corner. Turn sharp LEFT to follow the path down through heather towards a side valley containing a small reservoir. After an initial steep descent the path levels out and becomes a bridleway, passes a reservoir and continues down an enclosed track. When it meets another track, by your outward route, follow it LEFT down past a house to a track junction. Turn RIGHT back to the start.

For **Walk B** take the side path. Follow its right fork, soon descending into the side valley below. The delightful path continues down the attractive valley, later alongside walls, with a view of the reservoir below. At the left-hand corner of a facing wall, take a path bearing right down to join a bridleway at a waymarker post by the stream. Cross the plank bridge and follow the bridleway to pass the side of the reservoir and down to a gate. Follow the green track along the valley past two small reservoirs to the start.

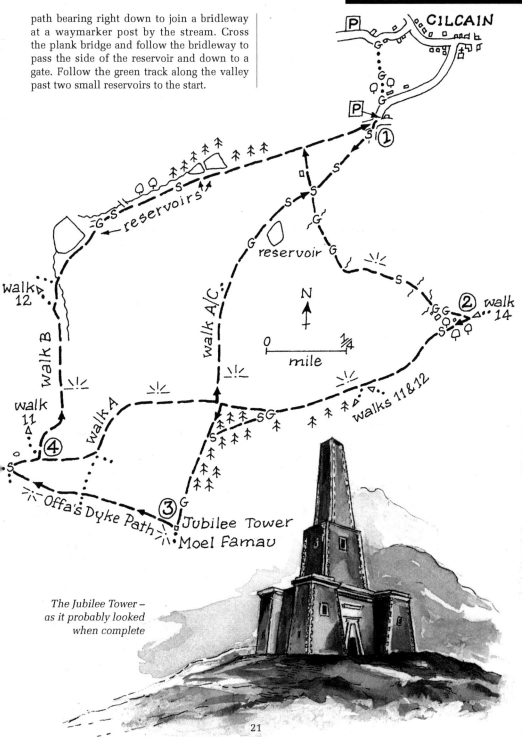

CILCAIN

walk 12

walk 14

walk B

walk A/C

reservoir

reservoirs

walk A

walk 11

N

0   ¼
mile

Offa's Dyke Path

walks 11 & 12

Jubilee Tower
Moel Famau

*The Jubilee Tower –
as it probably looked
when complete*

21

WALK 14

CILCAIN & THE ALYN VALLEY

DESCRIPTION A 7 mile walk (**A**) of much interest, exploring attractive valleys and foothills. The route takes you around Ffrith mountain, passes a medieval house, and visits the ancient hillside village of Cilcain, with its medieval church and 16thC coaching inn. It returns down the impressive wooded Alyn valley on the famous 'leete path', past limestone crags and old lead mines – scenery enjoyed by the writer Charles Kingsley and said to inspire Mendelssohn to write 'The Rivulet'. Allow about 4 hours. The route includes a shorter 4 mile walk (**B**). The 'leete path' can also be enjoyed as a 4 mile 'there and back' walk.

START Loggerheads Country Park Centre [SJ 198626] or Cilcain [SJ 172648].

DIRECTIONS The Country Park Centre lies on the A494 Mold-Ruthin road, 2 miles from Mold. See **Walk 13** for the alternative start.

*L*oggerheads *has been popular with visitors since the early 19thC. Crosville Motor Bus Company acquired land in 1926 and established tea-rooms, gardens, bandstand and boating lake for day-trippers. In 1974, it was established as a Country Park covering 74 acres of the Alyn valley and today offers a visitor centre and restaurant.*

Walk back along the drive, then at a house, take the signposted Moel Famau path on the right to a road. Follow it RIGHT. At a T-junction, turn RIGHT, then take the Moel Famau path through a gate on the left. Follow the green track along the attractive side valley, passing waymarked side paths. After about ½ mile, the track bends up towards a house and the Moel Famau path crosses a stile and a field corner to another stile. It continues to a ladder stile, then at a finger post, angles down to cross the stream.

2 Follow the fence on your right, and when it bends right, continue ahead to a waymarker post, from where the path briefly rises gently across the large field, passes another waymarker post and continues above a stream. In the right-hand field corner, cross the stream and a stile, then follow a bridleway to the far corner of a forest. (Here the Moel Famau path heads up through the trees.) Cross the stile ahead and follow the bridleway over a stream to a stile/gate and on past Brithdir-mawr – *a 16thC hall house*. Continue along the road, then after ½ mile, turn LEFT on a signposted bridleway to Moel Famau. (For **Walk B** continue down the road to a junction, then follow a waymarked path opposite down to cross the river, and go half-right up to join the leete path).

3 Follow the bridleway/track past Bryn Ffynnon and Llygad Yr Haul to a gate above Ffrith farm, past an alternative way-marked field path to Cilcain, then around the northern slopes of Ffrith Mountain. After a gate marked 'Castell', the bridleway splits. Take the RIGHT fork. The bridleway passes a cottage, then contours around the hillside – *offering good views to Cilcain* – before descending to cross a stream at a gate and continuing along an enclosed track. At a track junction, cross a stile on the right. Walk down the edge of two fields, then down a farm's access track to reach a nearby road. Follow it up into Cilcain.

*C*ilcain *is an ancient hillside settlement sited at a meeting point of old drover's roads. St Mary's 14thC church contains many interesting features, including a magnificent carved oak roof with winged angels. The White Horse, a 16thC coaching inn, and the last of seven village pubs, makes a good refreshment stop.*

4 At the crossroads by the inn, turn RIGHT, and follow the road down to take a signposted bridleway on the left down past troutpools. Near the stream, take a path angling up through the trees and on across the wooded slope to go through a fence gap. Turn RIGHT past young trees then follow the stiled field path above the wooded valley to eventually reach a road. Follow it down and across the river, then half-way up the hill, take a path on the right signposted to Loggerheads.

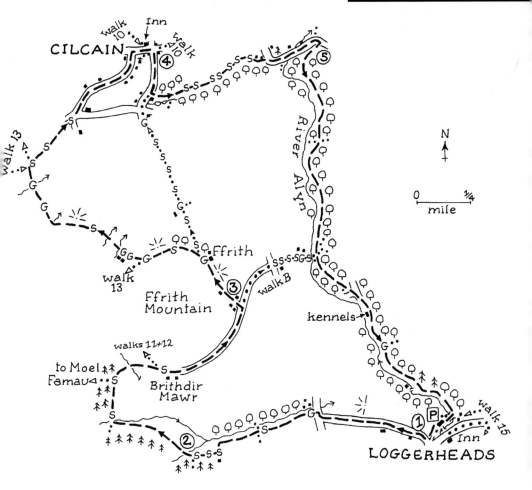

5 Now begins the delightful 'leete path' which takes you two miles along the beautiful Alyn gorge – a Site of Special Scientific Interest containing major cave systems – back to Loggerheads. The path takes its name from the distinctive 'leat' – *a water channel, originally 6 ft 6 ins wide and 5 ft deep, built in 1823 by Cornish mining engineer John Taylor, whose Mold Mines Company acquired lead mines in the area. Its purpose was to divert water from the river at Loggerheads past swallow holes in the limestone bed, into which the river disappears part of the year, to service waterwheels that powered mining machinery and waterpumps in the mines lower in the valley. It ceased to* operate in 1845. As you enjoy this tranquil valley it is hard to imagine the noise and activity generated during the 18th and 19th centuries when lead was extensively mined here. Keep with the level leete path high above the Alyn river, past limestone crags, impressive old lead workings, and through attractive woodland, to eventually cross a road. Go along a track, past Alyn kennels, and continue along the path, soon at river level. *On the opposite bank near a footbridge is the site of a 40 ft waterwheel installed in 1870 to work pumps at a mine on this side of the valley.* Cross a stone bridge over the river to return to the Centre

23

WALK 15
MOEL FINDEG & DEBORAH'S WELL

DESCRIPTION This 5 mile walk first heads south through Colomendy Outdoor Education Centre used by children from Merseyside, then Aberduna Nature Reserve to reach Maeshafn. It then rises through Moel Findeg Nature Reserve, comprising important lowland heath habitat fringed by woodland, to its summit (1194 feet) offering panoramic views. The return includes an ancient well with a tale to tell. There are a choice of country inns en route. Allow about 3 hours.

START Boundary stone monument at Loggerheads [SJ 202626].

DIRECTIONS From Mold take the A494 towards Ruthin. Just past Cadole, as the road descends, park on the left opposite a large boundary stone monument. Alternatively, park at Loggerheads Country Park Centre further down and walk back up the road to the start.

The boundary stone known as' Carreg Carn March Arthur' (the stone of the hoof of Arthur's horse) has an indentation said to be the hoof print made by King Arthur's magical horse Llamrei on landing after a mighty leap from Moel Famau to flee from a Saxon army. The monument above it was erected in 1763 to define the boundary, after a long dispute over mining rights between the lordships of Mold and Llanferres. This dispute inspired Richard Wilson – a renowned British landscape painter and a founder member of the Royal Academy, who spent his last years at nearby Colomendy Hall —to paint the original sign of the 17thC We Three Loggerheads inn. The sign showed the heads of two gentlemen back to back, as if each is refusing to speak with each other. The missing third 'loggerhead' – equivalent to 'blockhead' today – was meant to be the onlooker! The area takes its name from this famous sign.

1 Opposite the monument, take a path signposted to Maeshafn through the wood to cross a metal stile. Follow a track past outbuildings, then a lane past a house. At a junction bear LEFT towards the extensive buildings of Colomendy. (The next section is subject to an application to permanently divert the existing RoW (**B**) through Colomendy to the route created as a temporary diversion (**A**) which starts at a kissing gate on the right. If the diversion order is not made the original RoW will be well signposted to and through the wood.) The proposed route, signposted to Maeshafn and with kissing gates, follows waymarked field paths, then continues along the wood edge, soon bending up alongside a tall perimeter fence. At a gate in the fence it rejoins the original RoW and continues through Aberduna Nature Reserve, leaving it by a kissing gate. After passing Bryn Tirion, follow a track LEFT past two more houses to a road. Follow it up into Maeshafn with its 17thC Miner's Arms.

2 Continue through the village, then turn LEFT at a road junction. Shortly, turn RIGHT along a side road to enter Moel Findeg Nature Reserve – *created in 1999 following its purchase by the local authority with the help of villagers, who raised £100,000, to protect it from further quarrying.* Follow a path rising steadily through trees, later joining another path for a final climb up the more open hillside to cross a stile onto the summit. Continue along the ridge. At its rocky end, descend half-RIGHT to pass a telegraph pole then continue east, passing to the right of a group of trees ahead. Beyond a track leading left, angle LEFT down towards a farm to pass between gorse, then bear LEFT down to cross a stile in a fence corner. Go down the field to a stile/gate by the farm's pond and on to the road. Turn RIGHT, then at Haulfryn do a sharp U-turn along a track. Follow it to a gate and on past exposed limestone crags. After ⅓ mile cross a stile on the left. Head half-RIGHT across open ground, soon descending past old mine workings and stone supports to cross a stile near the left field corner. Follow a path down through the wood to a track by houses in Gwernymynydd. Turn RIGHT to reach the nearby A494 by the Rainbow Inn.

3 Cross the road to follow the signposted path along the track almost opposite. After a cattle-grid the track rises steadily —*soon offering extensive views over Mold and beyond* – then continues alongside a wood. Just before a gate and nearby house, cross a stile on the left. Follow the wall round to pass through a gate. Turn LEFT and follow the boundary down to cross a stile near the bottom corner by a pond. Follow

a path LEFT to a nearby lane. Follow it LEFT past bungalows, then take a waymarked short enclosed path on the right by Pathside cottage to a stile. Head across a large field, soon descending then rising to a stile in the left corner onto a road. Cross the stile opposite, and follow a path LEFT along the wood edge to Deborah's Well. *An engraved plaque records the tragic tale of Deborah, whose efforts in the 16thC to protect local people from cholera ironically led to her untimely end at the hands of those she sought to protect.*

4 Continue briefly along the wood edge, then turn RIGHT up a signposted path through the trees to a stile. The path continues besides a fence, rises, then bends LEFT and continues through the wood. After crossing a stile, keep ahead, soon steadily descending past side paths to reach a stony cross path. A nearby gate gives access to the Colomendy Arms in Cadole. Turn RIGHT and follow the path through a clearing past old workings and on to cross a stile. Continue through the wood, soon reaching a finger post. Here turn sharp LEFT down a wide path, past a seat – *and a path leading right back to Loggerheads Centre* – to reach the road by the start.

SOUTH OF LOGGERHEADS

DESCRIPTION A 4½ mile (**A**), 3¼ mile (**B**) or 2¼ mile (**C**) walk exploring the attractive part wooded countryside south of Loggerheads. The route passes through the edge of Glan-yr-Afon Hall estate and along a delightful section of the river Alyn. It then continues south past an attractive house, returning via Big Covert wood with a delightful bridleway to finish. Allow about 3 hours for the full walk.

START Loggerheads Country Park Centre [SJ 198626].

DIRECTIONS The Country Park Centre lies on the A494 Mold-Ruthin road, 2 miles from Mold.

*L*oggerheads *has been popular with visitors since the early 19thC. Crosville Motor Bus Company acquired land in 1926 and established tea-rooms, gardens, bandstand and boating lake for day-trippers. In 1974, it was established as a Country Park covering 74 acres of the Alyn valley and today offers a visitor centre and restaurant.*

I Return to the A494 then continue along the pavement past the garage and houses, then two entrances to Glan-yr-Afon hall. Just before the large road sign indicating the turning for Moel Famau, cross the road with care to take a signposted path over a stile. The path goes to a kissing gate, then rises up the field edge to another kissing gate. Follow the boundary on the left down past a cottage to a kissing gate and on past a wood to a kissing gate and stile in the corner. Follow the boundary on your right to cross the fast flowing stream by a waymarker post, then continue up the field edge alongside the stream to a kissing gate at the wood corner. Go half-LEFT to reach another kissing gate just beyond a bridge over the river. Follow the path through the wood, soon above the river, to another kissing gate. On the opposite bank is an old waterwheel. Follow the stiled riverside path to a nearby road.

2 Turn LEFT across the river. (For **Walk C** turn left along the side road.) Take the signposted path on the right through a gate at the end of Erw-Olchfa. Go past the side of the garage to a stile by the river, then follow the edge of two fields above the river to a stile in the corner. Now angle up the next field (waymarker misleading) to the far top corner by a wood. Go along the edge of the next field up to a stile. Angle up the field to the top corner by the attractive black and white house – *with views across the valley to Llanferres and Moel Famau.* Here turn RIGHT alongside the wall to a stile onto an access track. Cross the stile opposite and follow the path to another stile. A permissive path now rises past a corrugated barn to the house's access lane. Follow it up to a finger post at the entrance to Mount Pleasant Farm. (For **Walk B** take the path signposted to Maeshafn up the edge of the wood, past a waymarker post to reach a wide waymarked cross-path, where you rejoin the main route. Follow it LEFT (signposted to Maeshafn) and resume text at paragraph **4**.)

3 Follow the access track south to Mount Pleasant Farm. Just before the house, turn LEFT to go through the waymarked left of two gates at the wood corner above. Follow the path along the edge of the wood to a stile into the field. Continue ahead near the wood boundary, soon descending to cross a stile by a gate in its perimeter fence. Follow the wide path up through the wood to a waymarked cross-path. Turn LEFT and follow the waymarked path north towards Maeshafn through Big Covert wood, later being joined by Walk B.

4 After passing a cave on the left (do not enter) – *where an archaeological excavation in 1948/9 found evidence of early human occupation* – the wide path descends to a stile/gate. Continue ahead along the rough lane. Shortly, at a stile on the right turn LEFT and follow a path down through the trees to a cross-path. Follow it RIGHT to the gated entrance of a nearby house. Turn RIGHT along the track to a gate onto the nearby road. Go down the road then just beyond two houses on the left, take the higher of two signposted paths up a track on the right past a house to cross a makeshift stile by a waymarked gate.

5 Follow the tree boundary on the left round to cross a partly hidden stile in the corner. Keep ahead alongside the boundary, then after 50 yards go half-RIGHT past a telegraph pole to a waymarked gate onto an access track. Cross the stile opposite. Go down the field to a stile in the far corner onto a lane. Follow it RIGHT. Just after it bends right, follow the signposted bridleway past a house and on along the tree-lined track. At its end continue with the narrow enclosed bridleway, later with a view across to the limestone cliffs above Loggerheads and descending to cross a bridge over the river by a small lake. Cross the road with care then return to Loggerheads.

Bridge over the River Alyn

WALK 17

FRON HEN & BIG COVERT

DESCRIPTION A varied 5¾ mile walk exploring both sides of the Alyn valley near Llanferres, featuring contrasting open green hills and wooded limestone countryside. The route rises steadily to follow a delightful high-level bridleway round the open slopes of the foothill of Fron Hen, with excellent views, before descending to Llanferres, with its 18thC church and 17thC Inn. It then continues east to the lead-mining village of Maeshafn, with its 17thC inn, before passing through the attractive woodland of Big Covert. Allow about 3 hours. The route can easily be undertaken as two shorter circuits of 3 and 3½ miles.

START Lay-by on A494 Mold-Ruthin road ½ mile south of Llanferres [SJ 187598].

DIRECTIONS Heading towards Ruthin from Llanferres, the large lay-by is on the left, before the Llanarmon-yn-Ial turning.

1 From the Llanferres end of the lay-by, cross the road and go up the track opposite. At the farm entrance, continue ahead over a cattle grid to follow a rising track, which shortly passes another track on the right, then goes behind a house and chalets, before rising steadily up the edge of an attractive side valley. When the track finally reaches an open gateway and heads up towards a farm, continue straight ahead alongside a tree/wall boundary on a waymarked bridleway to go through a gate by the end of a wood. Go along the wood edge and at its end, turn RIGHT to follow a bridleway up alongside a wall to go through a small gate ahead. *The heather-covered hill up to your left is Moel Fenlli, with its Iron-Age fort.*

2 Continue up the track to pass through two further small gates above the farm, and follow the delightful gated bridleway round the open slopes of Fron Hen – *offering excellent changing views: south over the southern Clwydians to Llandegla Moors, Horseshoe Pass, Llantisilio Mountain and the*

Berwyns beyond; east to Eryrys mountain; and later, north east to Moel Findeg, Deeside, Merseyside, and, on a clear day, the distant Pennines. Shortly after a third gate, the bridleway bears RIGHT on a steady descent – later with a view of Moel Famau – to eventually pass through a gate by a house at a lane.

3 Immediately turn RIGHT over an adjoining stile, then contour around the mid-slopes, gradually moving away from the wall on your right, to pass the right-hand side of a corrugated barn. Go through several gates behind the farm. Continue ahead on a track past an area of gorse, and on alongside the fence on your left to descend to cross a stile at the bottom of a strip of forest. Keep ahead down the next field, alongside the fence and stream on your right, to cross the stream and stile in the field corner. Go round the base of the tree in front to follow a path across the field slope. Shortly, descend to a lower path to pass a waymarked post, and on alongside an old boundary above a house, then bend LEFT down to go through a gate. (For a shorter walk cross a nearby stile and follow a path down to the A494.) Now go down past the front of a house and follow the access lane down to the A494. Nearby is the 17thC Druid Inn, where refreshments are available, and the Church of St Berres, rebuilt in 1774.

4 Cross the road to a finger post opposite and go down a hedge-lined track (or for a shorter walk follow the road right back to the start). The track soon runs by, then crosses, the river Alyn to go through a gate ahead. Continue up the track to its end by stiles. Cross the stile on the left, then turn RIGHT along the field edge. In the corner, by the attractive black and white house, bend LEFT with the boundary. After about 100 yards angle away from the boundary to cross a ladder-stile ahead. Now follow a path through an area of shrubs and small

Fron Hen

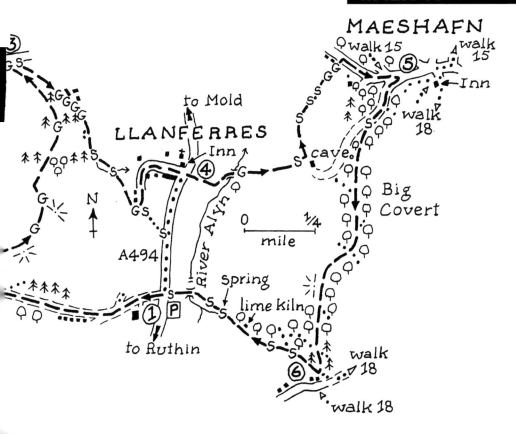

trees to cross a ladder-stile. Go across a small field, over another ladder-stile, then follow the boundary on your right round to pass through a gate. Now bear LEFT along the access track, on the waymarked path, through a gate, to reach the nearby road. Follow the road RIGHT up to Maeshafn.

5 Just after the 'Maeshafn' sign, do a 'U'-turn – *or first continue to the Miners Arms for refreshments* – to follow a sign-posted path to Bryn Alyn along a track to Pentre-cerrig-mawr through Big Covert wood. After a few hundred yards cross a second stile on the left by a gate. Follow the path through the wood. In about 200 yards, you will pass a cave hidden down on your right

– do not enter. An archaeological excavation in 1948/9 found evidence of early human occupation. Continue through the wood on the waymarked path (Bryn Alyn) past side paths to eventually descend to a track by a house.

6 Turn RIGHT on a path signposted to Plymog along the bottom edge of the wood. The stiled path continues past impressive limestone edges and an old lime kiln to a spring. After crossing the stream and a stile, go down the field edge, then head across the next field to cross a wide flat bridge over the river, then follow a track up to the start.

WALK 18

BRYN ALYN

DESCRIPTION A 6½ mile figure of eight walk (**A**) exploring the varied countryside between the old lead mining villages of Maeshafn and Eryrys. Highlights include impressive limestone scenery on Bryn Alyn, open pastureland, attractive woodland, an insight into local lead-mining, extensive views and the opportunity to visit two old country inns. Allow about 3½ hours. The route can easily be undertaken as a 3¾ mile walk (**B**) from Maeshafn and a 2¾ mile walk (**C**) from Eryrys.
START Maeshafn [SJ 202610] or Eryrys [SJ 204578].
DIRECTIONS Maeshafn is signposted from the A494 in Gwernymynydd. Park tidily in the village centre by the telephone box. For the Eryrys start see **Walk 19**.

*B**ryn Alyn**, rising to 1338 feet, known locally as Pothole Mountain, is a Site of Special Scientific Interest, and now designated Open Access land. It is renowned for its limestone grassland, pavements, escarpments, caves, and rich flora.*

I Head along the track past the 17thC Miners Arms – *where miners were once paid through a small window at its entrance* – and cottages. At its end by Pen-y-Ffordd continue ahead to cross a stile. Follow the fence on your right, then at a waymarker sign, go half-LEFT up to cross a stile in the field corner and another just ahead. Follow the boundary on your left past a small wood into the next field. (For an alternative route now angle up to a stile on the skyline. Follow the path to another stile and on past Burley Hill quarry, later bending away to rejoin the main route near a bungalow.) Otherwise, continue alongside the boundary up to cross a stile in the corner. Go over the remains of a wall and up the middle of the field to cross a stile. Go across the tree-lined slope ahead, then after 70 yards bear LEFT into an adjoining field. Head south towards a white bungalow to reach a ladder-stile just beyond.

2 Continue alongside the boundary, soon descending to cross a ladder-stile. Follow the path over rough ground to reach a road. Cross a stile opposite (signposted to Bryn Alyn) and follow the path up the hillside, later bending up steeper ground to cross a stile on the shoulder of the hill. Keep ahead across upland pasture to reach a way-marker post at a green track. Turn LEFT. (For **Walk B** turn right.)

3 Follow the track past an area of old lead workings to a road. Turn LEFT, then RIGHT along the access track to Fron Deg to cross a stile ahead. Continue ahead on a waymarked stiled path across five fields on Nercwys Mountain, then head half-LEFT, soon descending to enter the forest, with a lake nearby. Go half-LEFT through the conifers, and at another path turn RIGHT to the nearby ruin and information board about the 19thC East Pant Du leadmine. Turn RIGHT along a forestry track up to a waymarked cross-path. Turn RIGHT and follow the rising path to leave the forest by a stile.

4 Go across the field to cross a stile in the corner. Head half-LEFT to follow the boundary round to a stile – *offering good views to distant Arenig, Arans and Cader Idris.* Continue down a track for 40 yards, then cross a stile below. Go half-LEFT to join a track, which takes you to a lane. Follow it RIGHT down to a road. Turn LEFT to cross a stile on your right. Keep ahead, with the old boundary on your right to go through an old gateway, then head half-LEFT across the slope of a ridge round to cross a stile. Turn RIGHT along the field edge for 50 yards, then go half-LEFT to cross a stile/fence in the recessed corner and on over rough ground to a road. Follow it RIGHT into Eryrys. *Note the old village water pump opposite the Sun Inn.*

5 Continue ahead along Caer Odyn out of the village. Shortly, take a signposted path on the right by an old shed. Now follow the boundary on the left up the field, and after about 200 yards, angle away from the wall up the gorse and limestone covered hillside to cross a ladder-stile in the boundary to your right. *Here are extensive views south to*

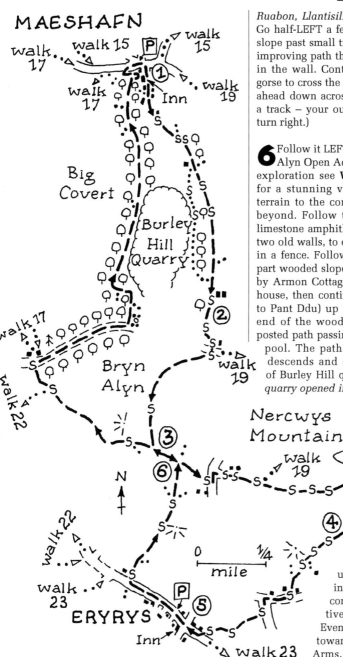

MAESHAFN

Ruabon, Llantisilio and Berwyn mountains. Go half-LEFT a few yards, then descend the slope past small trees. Now bear LEFT on an improving path through gorse to cross a stile in the wall. Continue ahead through more gorse to cross the bend of a green track. Keep ahead down across a grassy hollow to reach a track – your outward route. (For **Walk C** turn right.)

6 Follow it LEFT up to a stile to enter Bryn Alyn Open Access land. (For a suggested exploration see **Walk 23**.) Continue ahead for a stunning view across the limestone terrain to the contrasting green Clwydians beyond. Follow the track down through a limestone amphitheatre, over the remains of two old walls, to eventually cross a step-stile in a fence. Follow the path down the steep part wooded slope to a ladder-stile onto lane by Armon Cottage. Follow it RIGHT past a house, then continue on a track (signposted to Pant Ddu) up the wooded valley. At the end of the wood, turn LEFT on the sign-posted path passing two side paths at a deep pool. The path soon rises steadily, then descends and continues along the edge of Burley Hill quarry. *The huge limestone quarry opened in the late 1940s.* Keep with

the well waymarked undulating path, later moving away from the quarry and continuing through the attractive woodland of Big Covert. Eventually it bends right down towards the rear of the Miners Arms, then continues along the wood edge to the road which you follow RIGHT back to the start.

31

WALK 19
MOEL FINDEG

DESCRIPTION A 7 mile walk (**A**) through varied countryside with good views throughout. The route crosses the open pasture of Nercwys Mountain and woodland, later climbing to the summit of Moel Findeg (1194 feet) near Maeshafn. It was saved by villagers from the threat of quarrying and is now a nature reserve comprising important lowland heath habitat fringed by woodland. The route returns through attractive limestone country. There is a choice of three country inns en route (check opening times). Allow about 3½ hours. The route includes shorter 5¾ mile (**B**) and 2¾ mile (**C**) walks using link roads.
START Sun Inn, Eryrys [SJ 204578] or Maeshafn [SJ 202610].
DIRECTIONS At the cross-roads in Eryrys by the Sun Inn go along Caer Odyn, where there is road side parking on the right. For the alternative start see **Walk 18**.

I From the Sun Inn take the road towards Mold. Go past a side road, then cross a stile on the right just before a white cottage. Head half-LEFT, soon alongside a boundary to cross a stile. Go up the field and over the stile ahead, then bear LEFT alongside the tree boundary to cross a stile by a gate at a waymarked path junction. Go to another stile ahead, and on down rough pasture, later part gorse covered, to cross a stile in the bottom fence. Continue ahead over two further stiles, then head almost half-RIGHT up across the next field slope to cross a stile by a hidden small pool onto a lane.

2 Follow it LEFT. (For **Walk C** continue to the road at point **6**.) Shortly, go through the gateway of Coed Bach to a stile at the end of the garden. Follow a track through the wood to a stile. Go past a barn to a stile ahead. Go across the field, over another stile, then angle LEFT down to a stile in the corner. Continue ahead to cross a stile on your left. Just ahead, bear RIGHT along a path through gorse, then go half-LEFT to join a track. Follow it up to cross a stile at the near-

by gated entrance to a wooden chalet. Follow the path through the trees, soon descending to cross a stile. Bear RIGHT to follow the path through gorse to cross a stile. Follow the path to another stile. Now keep ahead to follow a waymarked path through woodland, over a stile, past a small pool and on through the forest, soon descending.

3 Near the the forest edge, at a waymarked path junction, turn LEFT and follow the forest track to a road. Turn LEFT, then RIGHT along the road towards Maeshafn. After about 200 yards, cross a stile on your right. (For **Walk B** follow the road to point **5**.) Keep ahead down the path and on through an old tree boundary, then go half-RIGHT to cross a ladder-stile. Go half-LEFT across the part tree/gorse/bracken covered slope to pass above a house. Keep ahead above its access track for about 40 yards, then angle up to nearby rough pastureland and pass round gorse, descending to rejoin the track at a gate. Cross the adjoining stile and follow the way-marked path to another stile and on to reach another access track. Cross the stile opposite, then follow the stiled path up to a road. Turn LEFT. (Turn right for the Owain Glyndwr Hotel.)

4 After passing Haulfryn, cross a stile on the left, go past a small pond, then go up the field to cross a stile in the right hand corner. Keep ahead and after 15 yards angle RIGHT on a path up the gorse-covered hill-side. Continue up across open ground, soon heading west and passing to the left of a small group of trees to eventually reach the small northerly rocky top of Moel Findeg – *offering panoramic views from the Pennines to Snowdonia.* Go along the short ridge, over a stile, then follow the path down. When it splits, take the LEFT fork, by a nearby pond. Follow the path across the wide top – *with views down to Maeshafn* – later descending to a road. Follow it RIGHT – *to the 17thC Miners Arms in Maeshafn if desired.*

5 Otherwise, just past the 'Maeshafn' sign, take a signposted path on the left along a driveway past Plas y Ffynnon to cross a stile. Turn LEFT and follow the boundary through two limestone meadows to cross a stile in the corner and another just ahead. Follow the boundary on the left through two fields up to cross a stile in the corner. Go over the remains of a wall and up the middle of the field to cross a stile. Go across the tree-lined slope ahead, then after 70 yards bear LEFT into the adjoining field. Head south towards a white bungalow and a ladder-stile just beyond. Continue alongside the boundary through trees, soon descending to cross a ladder-stile. Follow the path over rough ground to reach a road. Turn LEFT to a road junction.

6 Turn RIGHT along the road, then shortly, cross a ladder-stile on your right. Now head half-LEFT up open ground, later passing under cables and levelling out to cross a stile near the fence corner. Turn LEFT, cross the nearby track and continue across mined scarred ground, soon rising to cross the bend of a green track and on through gorse to cross a stone stile in a wall. Follow the meandering path through gorse to cross a visible ladder-stile in the wall on the right – *offering great views from Llandegla Moors to the distant Arans.* Head half-LEFT across open gorse and limestone covered ground down to a boundary wall, which you follow down to a lane by an old shed. Cross a stile almost opposite. Go up the field, over an old wall, then follow the boundary on your left to cross a ladder stile in the field corner. Continue ahead to cross another ladder-stile in the corner. Keep ahead for 30 yards, then bear LEFT through gorse to cross a stile in the field corner. Now go half-LEFT to cross a stile in the next field corner, and on between houses to a road. Follow it LEFT back to the start.

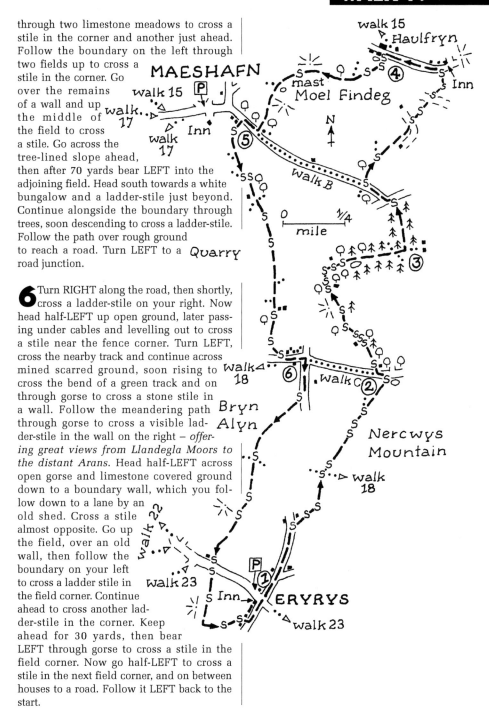

33

WALK 20
COED NERCWYS

DESCRIPTION A 2 mile waymarked multi-user circular trail around Coed Nercwys, with information boards at a good viewpoint, by the former Llyn Ochin, and at the site of a 19thC lead-mine. Allow about 1¼ hours.
START Car park, Coed Nercwys [SJ 218593].
DIRECTIONS From the A494 at Gwernymynydd, take the road to Maeshafn. At the junction turn left (brown tour sign). Follow the road to another junction. Turn right towards Eryrys, then take a minor road on the left opposite the road to Burley Hill quarry. Follow it for about ¾ mile to the forest car park. An alternative car park lies at the south western corner of the forest.

WALK 21
COED NERCWYS & BRYN ALYN

DESCRIPTION A 5¾ mile walk (**A**) featuring most of the Coed Nercwys trail and an exploration of the delightful limestone hill of Bryn Alyn, taking in its three small tops, offering panoramic views. A more direct 4 mile walk (**B**) from Coed Nercwys and a 2¾ mile walk (**C**) around Bryn Alyn from the Eryrys road (point 3) are also included.
START As **Walk 20**.

I Go through the gate and along the forestry track. Shortly, take the signposted trail angling off on the left. It rises through trees then continues through the open forest – *later with good views from Hope Mountain to Helsby*. At a path junction, keep ahead to follow the trail through the forest. Later it crosses a more open aspect to reach a forestry track. Follow it LEFT. Shortly, the trail turns RIGHT off the track and rises to an information board (**A**) at an excellent viewpoint. The trail continues through the forest, turns LEFT at a junction. Later it rises and diverts to an information board (**B**) by Llyn Ochin, now a marshy area. The trail continues north past a cross-path to reach an information board about the 19thC East Pant Du leadmine (**C**) by a ruin.

2 Continue along the trail. Soon angle RIGHT along a path to join a forestry track. Follow it LEFT down to the start.

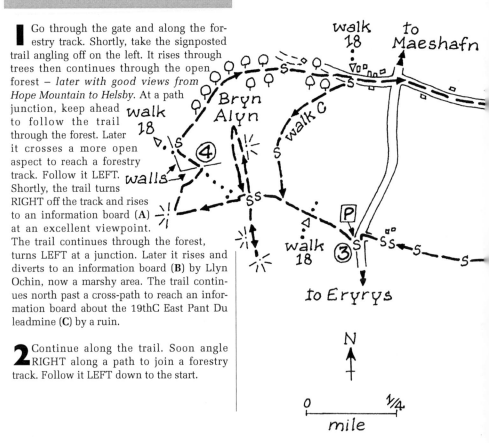

34

Bryn Alyn, rising to 1338 feet, known locally as Pothole Mountain, is a Site of Special Scientific Interest, and now designated Open Access land. It is renowned for its limestone grassland, pavements, escarpments, caves, and rich flora.

I For **Walk A** follow the circular trail instructions in paragraph **1** of **Walk 20** to the East Pant Du leadmine site (**C**). Here turn LEFT.

For **Walk B** go through the gate and along the forestry track. Go past the waymarked trail path and continue up the track. Shortly, take the waymarked trail path on the right to another track. Keep ahead to reach a ruin and an information board about the 19thC East Pant Du leadmine (**C**). Turn RIGHT.

2 After a few yards take a path on the left through conifers to cross a stile at the forest edge, with a pool nearby. Go half-LEFT

up the field to a ladder-stile, then follow the stiled waymarked path across several fields to Fron Deg and along its access track to the road. Turn LEFT. Take a path on the right signposted to Bryn Alyn (start of **Walk C**).

3 Follow the track up past old lead workings to eventually cross a stile into Bryn Alyn Open Access land. Cross another stile on the left and climb up to the first small top for panoramic all-round views: *from Snowdonia to the Pennines: from the Arans to the Lancashire coast. Continue south along the ridge for a good view of Eryrys.* Retrace your steps down to the stile. Turn LEFT briefly up the track then, turn RIGHT up the first limestone ridge to its highest point. Continue along the ridge to a fence. Here, do a sharp 'U'-turn to go along the edge of tussocky ground beneath the limestone escarpment, then follow a path along the top of a larger rocky escarpment back to the track. Continue down the track. When it bends down right, keep ahead alongside the fence, then follow a path up the slope ahead, passing through the middle of an impressive limestone pavement. Continue up to the highest point to enjoy commanding views across to the Clwydians. Head north along the ridge. Just before its end descend RIGHT to a path below. Follow it down to rejoin the track where an old wall crosses it.

4 Turn LEFT down the track. Just before it passes through another wall, angle RIGHT past a concrete stump to cross a hidden stile in a fence. Keep ahead on a delightful path, passing beneath a limestone escarpment, with a cave entrance above. The path soon passes above a wooded valley, then descends through trees, past an old mine entrance, to a stile. Keep ahead to follow a waymarked bridleway, soon rising above a house to join a road. (For **Walk C**, cross a stile on the right and follow the signposted Bryn Alyn path up the hillside, later bending up steeper ground to a stile, then continue ahead across upland pasture to rejoin the outward track.) At a crossroads follow the minor road ahead back to the start.

WALK 22

AROUND THE NANT

DESCRIPTION A delightful 5½ mile (**A**) or 5¼ mile (**B**) walk exploring the stunning limestone scenery north of Llanarmon-yn-ial, extensively mined for lead since the 13thC, and possibly in Roman times. This meandering walk passes a medieval castle and two of the area's few surviving mining relics, and visits Bryn Alyn Open Access area, offering extensive views. Walk A climbs to its western top (1322 feet). **Walk B** crosses its lower slopes. Allow about 3½ hours. A shorter 3 mile walk (**C**) is included.
START St Garmon Church, Llanarmon-yn-ial [SJ 191561].
DIRECTIONS In the village, go past the Raven Inn and the post office, to park on the roadside in Maes Ial.

*S*t *Garmon's is a medieval double-naved church, extensively restored during the 1730s, with many outstanding features.*

I Follow the B5431 back out of the village, soon crossing the river Alyn. *On the right is the remains of Tomen-y-Faerdre, the 11thC fortress home of the lords of Ial built on a natural rock outcrop. On the left is a large cave where prehistoric remains were found. The nearby farmhouse was once part of a medieval manor house.* Continue to the B5430. Turn LEFT, then RIGHT to follow the road towards Eryrys for ⅓ mile. After passing the Victorian primary school take a sign-posted path along a track on the left. When it splits keep ahead.

2 As the track bends down towards the farm, cross a stile by a gate ahead. Go down a green track to another stile/gate. Now follow the signed path up and through a gap in the tree boundary ahead, then across the small field to go through a hedge gap into a large field. Angle LEFT to join the boundary, descending to a gap in the old boundary ahead. Continue alongside the tree boundary on your left, soon passing through trees to cross a stile ahead. Go across the field, over

a stile, then descend to a lane. Go along the track opposite, past a house. At a track junction, bear LEFT up past a garage. *Here in the Nant, are a chimney flue and an impressive engine house, which once contained a steam engine used to pump water from the 19thC Great Westminster lead-mine. There was also a school here for miners' children.*

3 Just before a gate, turn LEFT up an enclosed path and follow it past Erw Nant. Follow its access track to a stile/gate by a cattle grid, then continue down another track. On the bend by The Cottage, cross a stile on the right. (For **Walk C** continue with the track to point **6**.) Go through a gate ahead, then bear LEFT with the boundary up through trees, soon reaching open ground. Continue up near the boundary, soon rising more steeply alongside a wall to reach a small limestone plateau. Keep alongside the wall to cross a stile in the corner below a transmitter mast. Follow the boundary on your right. After 25 yards, take a green track angling away from it, soon descending beneath the limestone escarpment and being joined by another track from a nearby lime kiln. Follow the track to go through a gate.

4 Turn LEFT along a tree-lined track. After a few hundred yards, before the track begins to descend, go through an old gateway on the right, then cross a stile ahead into Bryn Alyn Open Access land. Here you have a choice: For **Walk B** follow the boundary on the left, soon passing beneath limestone crags. From the boundary corner, the path continues across open ground. When it angles down follow a feinter path past two small trees ahead, then continue along a grass ridge, past an area of gorse, then descend towards a ladder-stile on the shelf below. Just before it turn LEFT to point **5**. For **Walk A** follow the path up the slope ahead, with a wall on your right. After 50 yards it bears LEFT near a fence then climbs steadily to the top of the limestone hill. Just before the end of the ridge, descend RIGHT to a path below. Follow it down to a track by a wall gap in the limestone amphitheatre. Follow it LEFT down the hillside. Just before a step-stile in a fence, turn LEFT up the wide grassy shelf. After passing a ladder-stile the ground levels out.

5 After passing another ladder-stile at a fence corner, keep ahead and go past a waymarked tree stump. Follow the path down the slope, past an old boundary corner, to a stile below onto the track left earlier. Follow it LEFT, and after about 300 yards, cross a stile behind a jutting out wall corner on the right. Follow the path to cross a ladder-stile. Now follow a path bearing LEFT, over an old wall and on up onto a small gorse covered top with extensive views. Turn RIGHT down a delightful green path, soon passing through gorse, then descending across the hillside to go through a gate by a bungalow. Continue along the lane.

6 Just beyond the access track to Bryn y Gwynt, turn LEFT along a signposted bridleway, passing in front of Bryn-y-Gloch and through a gate beyond. Follow the gated bridleway down to pass along the edge of the large quarry, and on down to the B5430. Take the enclosed path opposite, then at the caravan site entrance, turn RIGHT to cross a delightful stone bridge over the river Alyn, and on to cross a stile. Turn LEFT and follow the path round the edge of the large field up to cross a stile. Keep ahead by the hedge, over a stile and across the field to another stile ahead. Now go half-RIGHT up the next field to a stile in the corner by a garage/house. Follow the waymarked path to the 18thC Raven Inn.

LLANARMON·YN·IAL

WALK 23
LIMESTONE & LEAD

DESCRIPTION A 5¾ mile (**A**) or 4½ mile (**B**) walk exploring the attractive undulating countryside south of Eryrys, where lead-mining periodically flourished from the 18thC. The route includes a delightful section of upland limestone walking across Graig, a SSSI consisting of stepped limestone ridges, offering panoramic views – and relics of the area's lead-mining past. Allow about 3½ hours.
START Eryrys [SJ 204578].
DIRECTIONS See Walk 19.

*E*ryrys was built in the early 19thC in response to expanding lead-mining operations in the area, and at its peak, the parish, including Graianrhyd, boasted a population of over 1000. By the early 20thC the mines had closed.

I From the crossroads take the road signposted to Graianrhyd past the church. After a few hundred yards, take a signposted path through a gate on the right. Follow the boundary on the right up to a stile in the corner. Continue up to another stile, then follow the stiled path along the edge of three fields – *enjoying extensive views* – to reach a track. Follow it LEFT, soon rising to pass Bog Isa and a pool. Nearby was Bog mine – *at its peak, one of the biggest local lead-mines. Between 1925-38 spar (used mainly for pebble dashing houses) was extracted from its waste tips, and limestone removed.* At the top of a rise, keep ahead with the left fork down to a road. Follow it RIGHT.

2 Just before a house, take a signposted bridleway on the right. Follow it past an old chimney flue and mine entrance to a gate by a small pool. Continue with the delightful enclosed bridleway, later descending to a road. (For **Walk B** turn right, then just past Graig quarry, take a path on the left. Follow a green track up across open pasture, and on through a small wood to a stile by a house. Go through a gate ahead, then follow a path

ahead through trees, past a bungalow to the road. Turn right and resume text at point **4**.) For **Walk A** cross the road and follow it LEFT into Graianrhyd. At the far end of Maes Gwyn, take a signposted path over a stile on the right. Go along the field edge to cross a footbridge in the corner. Now go half-RIGHT across the field up to a stile, and on across the next field to a ladder-stile. Go up the slope ahead and on to pass through a gate. Go half-RIGHT across the next large field to the fence in the far corner by a large house. Follow it up through trees to cross a stile, then continue half-LEFT, soon descending to go through two gates onto a road. Turn LEFT.

3 After a few yards, cross a stile on the right, and follow the boundary on your left through a wettish reedy area to a stile in the corner. Follow the bottom edge of the gorse-covered slope of the next field to a stile onto a road. Follow it RIGHT for ¼ mile to go through the entrance to 18thC Allt Gymbyd Farm. Go past an outbuilding on your right, with the farmhouse to your left. Follow the waymarked path along a track past a large barn on the left, then between other barns to go through a gate. Keep ahead to cross a stile, then go along the field/golf link edge, soon descending to no. 2 golf tee to cross a ladder-stile just beyond. Continue along a long narrow field, following the tree-covered limestone ridge on your right to its end to reach a prominent waymarker post on the rise ahead. Turn RIGHT then follow the fence RIGHT round to cross a stile. Continue through a haulage yard, past an outbuilding and a house to a road. Turn LEFT.

4 After about 60 yards cross a ladder-stile set back on the left and follow a waymarked path beneath a tree-covered ridge. After an enclosed section of path, cross a ladder-stile and continue ahead down a narrow clearing to a gate by an outbuilding. Pass in front of the house, then bend RIGHT along its access track down to the road. Turn RIGHT. Shortly turn LEFT up a track opposite a side road. At the entrance to Pen-y-llwyn, continue ahead up a path to cross a stile by the house. Now follow an old wall on your right, rising steadily across the open

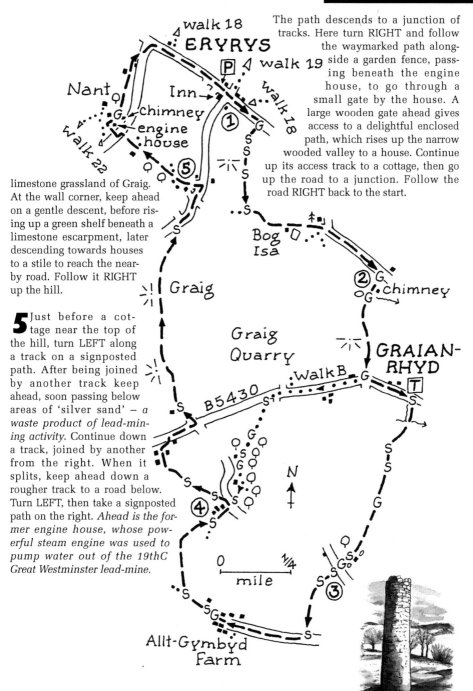

The path descends to a junction of tracks. Here turn RIGHT and follow the waymarked path alongside a garden fence, passing beneath the engine house, to go through a small gate by the house. A large wooden gate ahead gives access to a delightful enclosed path, which rises up the narrow wooded valley to a house. Continue up its access track to a cottage, then go up the road to a junction. Follow the road RIGHT back to the start.

limestone grassland of Graig. At the wall corner, keep ahead on a gentle descent, before rising up a green shelf beneath a limestone escarpment, later descending towards houses to a stile to reach the nearby road. Follow it RIGHT up the hill.

5 Just before a cottage near the top of the hill, turn LEFT along a track on a signposted path. After being joined by another track keep ahead, soon passing below areas of 'silver sand' – *a waste product of lead-mining activity.* Continue down a track, joined by another from the right. When it splits, keep ahead down a rougher track to a road below. Turn LEFT, then take a signposted path on the right. *Ahead is the former engine house, whose powerful steam engine was used to pump water out of the 19thC Great Westminster lead-mine.*

walk 18
ERYRYS
P ◁ walk 19
Nant
Inn →
walk 18
chimney
engine
house
walk 22
① G
⑤
S
Bog
Isa
② G chimney
Graig
Graig
Quarry
GRAIAN-
RHYD
T
Walk B
B5430
N ↑
④
0   ¼
mile
③
Allt-Gymbyd
Farm

PRONUNCIATION

These basic points should help non-Welsh speakers

Welsh	English equivalent
c	always hard, as in **c**at
ch	as on the Scottish word lo**ch**
dd	as th in **th**en
f	as f in o**f**
ff	as ff in o**ff**
g	always hard as in **g**ot
ll	no real equivalent. It is like 'th' in **th**en, but with an 'L' sound added to it, giving '**thlan**' for the pronunciation of the Welsh 'Llan'.

In Welsh the accent usually falls on the last-but-one syllable of a word.

KEY TO THE MAPS

- **→** Walk route and direction
- ▬ Metalled road
- = = = Unsurfaced road
- • • • • Footpath/route adjoining walk route
- ∿→ River/stream
- ♣ ↷ Trees
- ▬■▬ Railway
- **G** Gate
- **S** Stile
- **F.B.** Footbridge
- ⟍⟋ Viewpoint
- ⟦P⟧ Parking
- ⟦T⟧ Telephone

THE COUNTRY CODE

Be safe – plan ahead and follow relevant signs

Leave gates and property as you find them

Protect plants and animals, and take your litter home

Keep dogs under close control

Be considerate to other people

Open Access

Whilst most routes follow public rights of way or established permissive paths, some cross areas of land where walkers have the legal right of access under The CRoW Act 2000 introduced in May 2005. Open Access land is detailed on OS Explorer 265 map. This access can be subject to restrictions and closure for land management or safety reasons for up to 28 days a year. Please respect any notices. The Countryside Council for Wales website (www.ccw.gov.uk) provides updated information on any closures.

Useful telephone numbers:

Denbighshire Countryside Services: 01352 810614

Denbighshire Highways Department: 01824 706872

Flintshire Highways Department: 01352 701233/4

traveline cymru: 0871 200 22 33

Denbighshire Bus Services: 01824 706968

Published by
Kittiwake
3 Glantwymyn Village Workshops,
Glantwymyn, Machynlleth, Montgomeryshire
SY20 8LY
© Text and map research: David Berry 2009
© Maps & illustrations: Kittiwake 2009
Drawings by Morag Perrott
Cover photographs: David Berry – *Main*: View from
Bryn Alyn towards Moel Famau. *Inset*: Old lead
mine, near Graianrhyd.

Care has been taken to be accurate. However neither the author nor the publisher can accept responsibility for any errors which may appear, or their consequences. If you are in doubt about any access, check before you proceed.

Printed by MWL, Pontypool.
First edition: 2000. Revised reprint: 2002
New edition: 2005. New extended edition 2009

ISBN: 978 1 902302 70 6